Interfaith Leadership

BOOKS BY EBOO PATEL

Acts of Faith: The Story of an American Muslim,
the Struggle for the Soul of a Generation

Sacred Ground: Pluralism, Prejudice,
and the Promise of America

Building the Interfaith Youth Movement:
Beyond Dialogue to Action (edited with Patrice Brodeur)

Interfaith Leadership

A Primer

Eboo Patel

BEACON PRESS
BOSTON

BEACON PRESS
Boston, Massachusetts
www.beacon.org

Beacon Press books
are published under the auspices of
the Unitarian Universalist Association of Congregations.

Printed in the United States of America

19 18 17   8 7 6 5 4

This book is printed on acid-free paper that meets the uncoated paper
ANSI/NISO specifications for permanence as revised in 1992.

Text design and composition by Kim Arney

Library of Congress Cataloging-in-Publication Data
Names: Patel, Eboo, author.
Title: Interfaith leadership : a primer / Eboo Patel.
Description: Boston : Beacon Press, 2016. | Includes bibliographical
    references and index.
Identifiers: LCCN 2016003604 (print) | LCCN 2016012876 (ebook) |
    ISBN 9780807033623 (pbk. : alk. paper) | ISBN 9780807033630 (ebook)
Subjects: LCSH: Leadership—Religious aspects. | Religions—Relations.
Classification: LCC BL65.L42 P38 2016 (print) | LCC BL65.L42 (ebook) |
    DDC 201/.5—dc23
LC record available at http://lccn.loc.gov/2016003604

to the people in the middle, building

Democracy, in its essence and genius, is imaginative love for and identification with a community with which, much of the time and in many ways, one may be in profound disagreement.

—MARILYNNE ROBINSON,
"Imagination and Community"

Contents

What Is Interfaith Leadership?

Ruth Messinger, the former president of the American Jewish World Service, has a powerful story of interfaith leadership. She grew up in an observant Jewish home in New York City, attended Radcliffe College in the early 1960s, married, and started seeking a way for her (then) husband to avoid the Vietnam War. His best option was finding work as a doctor in a government facility. They tried getting a position in a major city on one of the coasts, but somehow wound up being assigned to a small town in Oklahoma. Ruth decided to make the most of an unfamiliar situation and enrolled in the master's program in social work at the University of Oklahoma.

After completing her degree in 1964, Ruth took a job as the director of child welfare programs for two counties in western Oklahoma. She quickly discovered that what passed for children's services in the area was an ugly collusion between the sheriff and Ms. Lucy, a woman who ran a ramshackle orphanage. Children and teenagers caught running away from home or committing minor crimes were thrown into jail and then sent to Ms. Lucy's orphanage. Ruth's first order of business was to inform the sheriff that putting a minor into jail was illegal. Moreover, Ms. Lucy's "facility" was totally unfit for children. If the minor's family was indeed unsuitable, the state had to provide an appropriate foster home for the child.

The sheriff's quick retort was that there were no foster homes in the area, and thus his was the only game in town. Then he lit into Ruth. She was clearly not from around here, she was a woman, and—to top it all off—she was Jewish. She could go take a hike.

Ruth knew that part of what the sheriff was saying was true; there were no foster homes in the area for the youth who needed them. Her job was not just to end the terrible current practice; it was to create a better alternative. She started going for walks around various neighborhoods in her town to get to know the area better, pushing a stroller with her newborn baby inside. She noticed that many of the private residences were marked with religious signs like "The Church of Jesus Christ Who Died for Our Sins."

Ruth knocked on doors and began conversations with the people who answered. She introduced herself and explained that her job was to help vulnerable children in western Oklahoma. She detailed the challenges facing troubled youth in the area and expressed that her highest hope was to help those kids find loving homes. Based on the religious sign she had seen outside the house, it looked like the residence doubled as a place for worship and community gathering. Might they help?

The most common response went something like this: "Come back on Wednesday morning for our praise service and speak to the group."

There seemed to be some kind of religious gathering taking place at one house-church or another just about every day of the week and just about every hour of the day. Ruth sat through countless sermons, praise songs, and altar calls. As promised, the preacher would give her a chance to speak. Ruth would rise and tell stories of local children and teenagers in need. When she was done, the preacher would quote scripture and say to the gathered worshippers, "Who here will answer the call of God and serve as loving families for these young people?"

"People would literally line up to help," Ruth said. "It was amazing to witness. Those evangelical house-churches built the child welfare network in western Oklahoma."

I found one particular story that Ruth told especially moving. Every few weeks or so, Ruth would get a call from the sheriff in the middle of the night. As the number of foster families in the area grew, he had grudgingly stopped his practice of throwing troubled youth in jail and carting them off to Ms. Lucy's facility. Instead, when he caught a runaway in the middle of the night, he phoned Ruth. "If you can't find a home for this kid within the hour, she's going to jail," he would say in his gruff voice. Without getting out of bed, Ruth would phone her friend Stacy, a devout evangelical who had told Ruth that she felt called by God to do whatever she could to help youth in need. Ruth would explain the situation, and Stacy would say, "Have the sheriff drop the girl off at my house." Ruth relayed the message to the sheriff. Stacy would meet the child at the door with a cup of hot cocoa, make her feel comfortable, and give her a bed for the night. Ruth would show up the next morning to work out a long-term solution.

Even as things got better, they were far from easy. Part of this had to do with Ruth's being Jewish in a time and place rife with anti-Semitism. Ruth recalls riding in a car with a group of older women when one of them said that she was off to do her shopping and aimed to "Jew down" the prices. She also remembers the day her colleagues at work found out that she was Jewish. She was met with surprised looks and a comment from her boss: "Well, you don't look Jewish." Many of the things that she heard in local churches contradicted her faith; some even offended her. One time, she was invited to a Sunday morning service at one of the fancier churches in town. It turned out to be Palm Sunday, and the pastor gave a fiery sermon on the killing of Jesus— by Jews.

Ruth was deeply offended and resolved to use the moment as an opportunity for education. She invited the pastor over to her home for tea and what we would now call an interfaith conversation. Ruth shared that not only was the pastor factually wrong about his claim that Jews killed Jesus, but that she was Jewish and felt hurt and insulted by his sermon. Moreover, America was growing increasingly religiously diverse. Sermons like the one he just gave were sure to cause division. And then Ruth pointed out a powerful area of commonality between her faith and his: Jesus was Jewish. Instead of preaching insulting and divisive falsehoods, why not focus on how the actions of Jesus inspired both Jews and Christians to serve others?

Just as Ruth helped the Christians she worked with understand Judaism, so she developed a deeper appreciation for evangelical Christianity during her time in western Oklahoma. She was especially struck by the ethic of service in the community: "They preached that God meant for us to serve others, and they practiced what they preached. When the pastor asked for volunteers and quoted scripture, people lined up to help."

The 1960s were a tumultuous time—the women's movement, the counterculture, the protests against the Vietnam War. Ruth Messinger and those evangelicals in western Oklahoma lined up on different sides of most of those major issues. Ruth was a graduate school–educated liberal Jewish feminist from New York who found herself in Oklahoma because her husband was fleeing the Vietnam War. The evangelicals she was working with helped make Merle Haggard's "Okie from Muskogee," with its lyrics celebrating a traditional understanding of American patriotism (against draft-dodging; for waving the flag on Main Street), one of the most popular songs of the era. Suffice it to say there were significant differences between Ruth and the majority of her evangelical partners on most of the issues of the time.

Yet Ruth identified a powerful point of intersection between their evangelical Christian values and her Jewish values. At the heart of that intersection was the welfare of young people from troubled family situations in western Oklahoma. There are hundreds in western Oklahoma who lived in loving homes rather than a derelict orphanage because of Ruth.

Ruth's story exemplifies the kind of interfaith leadership I focus on in this book. Interfaith leaders are people who have the ability to lead individuals and communities that orient around religion differently toward understanding and cooperation. This book makes a case for why this work is important and provides a guide for how to do it effectively. To that end, it is useful to say a few more words about how Ruth's story illustrates this kind of interfaith leadership.

Ruth sought connection rather than division. When she saw Christian signs outside of people's homes, her instinct was not "I disagree with that understanding of Jesus, therefore I am staying away from that house." Instead, she thought to herself, "That is clearly a place where a leader lives and people gather. I will certainly have differences and disagreements with them, but we will also likely have some deeply held values in common. I will work to find those shared values and highlight them in a way that inspires all of us to create a foster-care network for youth."

It is one thing to seek connection; it is another thing to have the skills to successfully connect. Ruth found ways to speak to and mobilize a different religious community for a common cause. She learned to build trust with the pastor. She learned to earn goodwill by paying personal visits to house-churches and spending time with the people who gathered there. She even learned that being a new mother with a little baby provided an initial point of positive contact.

Ruth had significant disagreements with her evangelical partners. She did not agree with them about their doctrine of Jesus as Lord and Savior, or their support for the Vietnam War, or their dim view of feminism. Ruth did not attempt to erase those disagreements, nor did she let the disagreements prevent her from partnering with them on finding foster homes. When the disagreement crossed the line into insult, she addressed the situation head-on, as with the Palm Sunday sermon on Jews killing Jesus. Crucially, she used the situation as an opportunity to educate her interlocutor, not simply scold him. Her method of education was to highlight something shared between their different traditions, namely, that Jesus was Jewish.

Even as Ruth was educating those around her about Judaism, her own knowledge about and appreciation for evangelical Christians grew. She admired their strong sense of community and their deep belief in God and, most of all, that they preached the importance of service and practiced what they preached.

CIVIC INTERFAITH LEADERSHIP

Ruth's story illustrates the central focus of this book, what I am calling "civic interfaith leadership in a religiously diverse democracy." The term "interfaith leader" typically conjures up images of old men dressed in official regalia, invested with formal religious authority, debating doctrine in fancy cathedrals. Ruth was not a theologian, a pastor, or an elderly man. She was a young, female social worker who had the ability to engage house-churches and government agencies, pastors and sheriffs, religious doctrine and federal laws, to benefit the lives of a vulnerable youth population. The where, who, and what of civic interfaith leadership certainly includes churches, clergy, and doctrine, but that is a relatively narrow slice of the broader landscape that I intend the word "civic" to convey.

When I use the term "civic interfaith landscape," I mean the various spaces (schools, parks, college campuses, companies, organizations, libraries, sports leagues, hospitals) where people who orient around religion differently interact with one another with varying degrees of ignorance and understanding, tension and connection, division and cooperation, *when their faith identities are implicated by that interaction.* When I say "civic interfaith work," I mean the kinds of activities and conversations that, through addressing diverse faith identities in interaction, strengthen a religiously diverse democracy. An interfaith leader is someone expert in organizing these.

Sometimes an interfaith leader has to respond to interfaith dynamics that emerge somewhat surprisingly in a civic space. Take, for example, the funeral arrangements that followed the tragic killing of Officer Wenjian Liu, believed to be the first Chinese American in the New York Police Department to be killed in the line of duty.[1] NYPD officials are accustomed to organizing Roman Catholic funerals involving thousands of uniformed officers and solemn eulogies by dignitaries. Officer Liu was part of a Buddhist tradition that commemorates death very differently. An auspicious day must be chosen for the event, rather than simply a day that is convenient for the public officials who wish to speak. There is generally no eulogy celebrating the life of the departed. In fact, a Chinese Buddhist funeral is typically not a public affair at all. Relatives and close friends gather in a private setting with Buddhist monks and wail, sob, and fall to the ground throughout the somber prayer ceremony. They burn objects signifying affluence in front of a picture of the deceased so that he may be comfortable in the afterlife. This approach, favored by the family, made little room for the many police officers who understandably wanted to pay tribute to their fallen brother in a manner ritually meaningful for them. Whoever it was at the NYPD who actually organized the funeral must have had some interfaith leadership skills.

Other times, an interfaith leader will seek to enrich a civic space by proactively mobilizing interfaith networks. If you are an active citizen and a community volunteer in an American suburb and the mayor asks you to pull together a thousand people for a major blood drive, you will no doubt want to tap into the social capital of local faith communities. And once you've got them together at an event they feel is an expression of their various faith commitments to serve others, you might want to use the opportunity to organize an interfaith discussion and have them share stories about how their faith inspires them to help others. You will need to figure out how to be inclusive of Jehovah's Witnesses and other faith communities who are religiously opposed to blood transfusions. Such a scenario highlights one of the great challenges of interfaith leadership—how to navigate the many areas in which people who orient around religion differently disagree.

RELIGIOUSLY DIVERSE DEMOCRACY

The different ways that people express religious and secular identities are especially important in a democracy, where people are free to bring their personal convictions into public life. In a democracy, people have the power of speech, association, and election. You can build institutions that gather people of like beliefs and, through these, amplify your voice. You can make that voice heard in politics by voting for particular candidates or running for office yourself. In this way, you can influence budgets and write laws. And if you come across a law that you feel infringes on your religious identity, you can file a case in court.

American democracy affords a special place to religious identity. It is not for nothing that the British writer G. K. Chesterton said that "America is a nation with the soul of a church."[2] The Puritans who arrived in Massachusetts Bay in the seventeenth century came seeking religious freedom. The founders had much to say about this freedom, including what they wrote in the First Amendment. Subsequent generations have strengthened this notion of special privilege for religion, most notably in the Religious Freedom Restoration Act of 1993 and the Supreme Court's decision in the *Hobby Lobby* case.[3] Moreover, American society is far more religious in just about every respect than other industrialized nations.

Given all this, it should come as no surprise that the place of religion in a diverse democracy has been a central topic of discussion among political philosophers. Some, like John Rawls, saw the thriving of religious diversity in democratic cultures as a significant challenge. His term for religion was "comprehensive doctrine."[4] He was concerned that a religious person has a comprehensive doctrine very different from the comprehensive doctrine that Rawls believes ought to underpin a liberal democracy. How can we be sure that said religious person will give his allegiance to the underlying arrangements of a liberal democracy, for example, to the president rather than the pope? How are we to know that if a particular religious group gains power, it will not attempt to force its religiously based positions through the mechanisms of government, thus imposing its comprehensive doctrine on others?

Religious diversity complicates matters further because it means there are multiple comprehensive doctrines in a single society. How can we be sure that people from those diverse communities will be intelligible to one another? After all, they do not share the same views with regard to creation, salvation, religious authority, and so on. For Rawls, the problem of potential tribalism only compounded the initial problem of misplaced loyalty. Religious diversity in a democracy may well give rise to conflict between religious groups that collectively have no regard for the authority of the government or the legitimacy of its basic political arrangements.

Rawls's famous solution to the problem is to suggest religious discourse be limited to the private sphere and kept out of political discourse.[5] Citizens, especially those acting in political roles, are free to practice their faith at home, but they ought not bring it into the public square. They should not, for example, offer religious reasons for their political positions. Their views on civil rights, antipoverty efforts, abortion, foreign aid, and so on should be expressed in the terms of what Rawls calls "public reason," which is rooted in the social contract of a liberal democracy and is by definition devoid of religious language. Rawls allows for religious reasons only if they are quickly followed by justifications consistent with his notion of public reason.

Not surprisingly, religious philosophers have taken issue with this position. Nicholas Wolterstorff, for example, writes:

> It belongs to the religious convictions of a good many religious people in our society that they ought to base their decisions concerning fundamental issues of justice on their religious convictions. They do not view as an option whether or not to do so. It is their conviction that they ought to strive for wholeness, integrity, integration, in their lives: that they ought to allow the Word of God, the teachings of the Torah, the command and example of Jesus, or whatever, to shape their existence as a whole, including, then, their social and political existence. Their religion is not, for them, about something other than their social and political existence; it is also about their social and political existence. Accordingly, to require of them that they not base their decisions and discussions concerning political issues on their religion is to infringe, inequitably, on the free exercise of religion.[6]

Wolterstorff is making a basic point not just about religion, but also about democracy. Citizens of a democracy are free to base their views on whatever they want and express them (within broad limits) however they wish. If this gives rise to tension between those groups or calls for political change, that is part of the process of democracy. Moreover, American democracy has benefited greatly from precisely this dynamic. Consider how both the abolitionist and civil rights movements involved a public religiosity that caused tension with other groups and sought fundamental political change.

Still, Wolterstorff gives short shrift to Rawlsian concerns about what Justice Felix Frankfurter called "cohesive sentiment."[7] Isn't it possible that encouraging people with very different religious convictions to express those identities in public might lead to protracted violent conflict, or at least a society where people are living in separate and mutually unintelligible religious universes?

The Princeton philosopher Jeffrey Stout offers a solution. Stout agrees with Wolterstorrf that people have a right to express themselves, but he takes seriously Rawls's concern with the cohesive whole and the arrangements that underlie it. Yes, people ought to express themselves, but they should express themselves with the hope of being intelligible and convincing to one another, and they should direct significant energy to the health of the whole. Such practices strengthen what Stout calls the "civic nation."[8]

Stout sees this civic nation as sacred, defined as the American people rather than the American government. He believes that the ties that bind a cacophonous country of 320 million into a civic nation with a collective destiny are energetic civic activities, activities he refers to as "thick democratic practices." Only by playing soccer and baseball, forming block clubs and PTAs, and most importantly, by listening and talking to one another with candor and sympathy, can we have any hope of building understanding and cooperation across diverse identities. Above all, a democratic people, a civic nation, is a community of citizens who can offer intelligible reasons to one another for their political views and public positions. Stout writes: "[Democracy] takes for granted that reasonable people will differ in their conceptions of piety, in their grounds for hope, in their ultimate concerns, and in their speculations about salvation. Yet it holds that people who differ on such matters can still exchange reasons with one another intelligibly, cooperate in crafting political arrangements that promote justice and decency in their relations with one another, and do both of these things without compromising their integrity."[9]

Religion is about fundamental things. Diversity is about people with different identities and deep disagreements interacting with great frequency and intensity. Democracy is about the freedom to advance your deepest personal convictions in public life. In a religiously diverse democracy, especially one that accords a special place to faith, deep disagreements on fundamental matters are to be expected. A healthy religiously diverse democracy is a society where people who disagree on some fundamental things do so without violence and in a manner where they are still able to work together on other fundamental things.

An interfaith leader is someone who can create the spaces, organize the social processes, and craft the conversations such that people who orient around religion differently can have a common life together.

WHY LEADERSHIP?

In a classic article for *Harvard Business Review* titled "What Leaders Really Do," John Kotter writes, "Change is the function of leadership."[10] But in the Internet era, why do we need leaders to effect change? Doesn't change happen at the click of a button or the move of a mouse or the speed of a tweet? Actually, recent research shows that the most important driver of certain types of change is an effective leader. A story told by Atul Gawande in the *New Yorker* illustrates.[11]

In the late 1960s, medical researchers discovered a simple solution for combating diarrheal diseases like cholera: drink ten to twenty liters a day of a fluid with a particular mixture of sugar and salt. A few years later, this solution was found to dramatically reduce deaths related to cholera during an outbreak in Bangladesh. Some public health officials assumed that the next steps were easy—simply publicize the beneficial effects of the mixture and advertise them in a public education campaign. The recipe was simple, the materials were readily available, and the stakes could not be higher.

For all its easy logic, the public education campaign failed. Turns out there was no great demand for a simple, lifesaving cholera solution, even after publicizing how well it worked. Death rates due to diarrheal disease remained stubbornly high in Bangladesh.

A decade later, a Bangladeshi organization called BRAC attempted an alternative approach. BRAC hired teams of people, trained them to teach those caught in the grip of cholera how to make and use the lifesaving solution, and then sent them out to affected villages across Bangladesh. In the course of their work, the teams learned the art of convincing desperate mothers that the best thing to do for a wailing baby emitting streams of fluid from both ends of his body was to *keep giving him this nasty-tasting solution.* The teams went through four thousand villages, taught the process to twelve million families, and saved a stunning number of lives.

In a digital age, it is tempting to think that technical fixes are all that are needed to spur social change, especially in situations where the problem is dire and the solution is fairly straightforward. But, as the Bangladesh cholera story illustrates, there's frequently an old-school dynamic to social change. It's not a cool website or a sexy public relations campaign that ultimately bends the arc; it's a person. As Gawande puts it: "In the era of the iPhone, Facebook and Twitter, we've become enamored of ideas that spread as effortlessly as ether. We want frictionless, 'turnkey' solutions to the major difficulties of the world—hunger, disease, poverty. We prefer instructional videos to teachers, drones to troops, incentives to institutions. People and institutions can feel messy and anachronistic."[12]

Gawande reminds us that there are actually many areas where real people are the key drivers of social change. We rely on teachers in our schools to teach our kids. The US government has sent out hundreds of thousands of agricultural extension agents to help farmers learn the most effective methods for improving crop yields. Theoretically, those things could have been left to ad campaigns, books, and websites. But the fact is, in many areas, people learn best from other people.

Social change is essentially a process of getting people to do things differently, something scholars call "creating new norms." As Everett Rogers, the social change guru and author of the highly influential book, *Diffusion of Innovations*, writes, "Diffusion is essentially a social process through which people talking to people spread an innovation."[13]

Gawande, building on Rogers's statement, concludes, "People follow the lead of other people they know and trust when they decide whether to take up [something new]. Every change requires effort, and the decision to make that effort is a social process."[14]

People change when they are taught by other people whom they find relatable and inspiring. The people who do the teaching, the relating, and the inspiring we call leaders. Interfaith leaders are people who cause other people to change their attitudes and actions with respect to religious diversity.

LOCATING MYSELF

The personal identities and commitments each of us brings to interfaith leadership will most certainly color our work. That is as it should be. An interfaith leader need not check her identity at the door, but does need to be aware of how her various views and positions might affect her engagement in any particular situation.

Let me take myself as an example. As I was writing the story about Ruth Messinger, I realized that I couldn't name a single evangelical pastor who runs a house-church in Oklahoma, but I have dozens of friends like Ruth. My own position as a Chicago-based, broadly progressive, Oxford-educated Ismaili Muslim who leads a nonprofit organization puts me in circles where I am far more likely to be in relationship with highly educated, city-dwelling, liberal Jews who run civil society organizations than with evangelical pastors leading house-churches in western Oklahoma. I know how Ruth tells the story of working with those evangelicals to build a foster-care network, but I don't know how those evangelicals tell it.

My identity shapes my world and my worldview—my network of relationships, the stories I am likely to hear, and the manner in which I am likely to filter them. Therefore, it most certainly shapes this book. One obvious way is the examples I use. Most of the illustrations in this book come from the religious traditions with which I am familiar, the world of higher education (based both on my experience speaking at over one hundred campuses and on my familiarity with the writings of certain scholars) and my regular diet of reading (the *New York Times, New Yorker, Atlantic*). The frameworks I present here emerge out of these experiences. My hope is that you are able to place your own experience within the categories I articulate. In other words, when I illustrate the theology of interfaith cooperation with Muslim stories, I hope that you are able to place your own stories coming from your own Catholic or Hindu or humanist identity within the framework that I present. If you find that your world and worldview lead you to articulate substantially different frameworks on any of the questions that I address here, I hope you write your own book. That is precisely how the process of defining the field of research, teaching, and practice that is interfaith leadership will progress.

ABOUT THIS BOOK

As a primer, the book is meant to be a relatively clear and quick read. It is intended for faculty who teach classes that deal with religious diversity, and students open to a meaningful twenty-first-century vocation; for participants in the growing number of interfaith groups across the nation and the world; for citizens of small towns, suburbs, and cities who are watching their patch of earth grow ever more diverse and are committed to making the most of an opportunity both civic and sacred; and for members of faith or philosophical communities with an increasingly wide array of friends and family members who orient around religion differently and who want to both articulate their perspective on ultimate concerns and have good relationships with those who have other views.

This book has seven chapters, corresponding to the six categories that I think are essential for interfaith leadership: identity, theory (this category has two chapters), vision, knowledge base, skill set, and intangible qualities.

Chapter 1, "The Identity of an Interfaith Leader," explores how people can mine personal experience to create a narrative identity as an interfaith leader.

Chapters 2 and 3 are about the theory of interfaith. I break the term "interfaith" into its component parts, "inter" and "faith." "Inter" is defined as the relationships between people who orient around religion differently. "Faith" is defined as the relationship between an individual and what we commonly understand as a religious or philosophical tradition (such as Christianity, Hinduism, or humanism). The term "interfaith," therefore, has two profound implications: how do our relationships with those who are different affect our relationships with our religious or philosophical traditions, and how do relationships with our traditions affect how we interact with people who are different from us?

Chapter 4, "The Vision of Interfaith Leadership," presents frameworks that flesh out what interfaith leaders hope their efforts will achieve.

Chapter 5 is on the knowledge base required for interfaith leadership.

Chapter 6 enumerates the skill set needed to be an effective interfaith leader.

Chapter 7 highlights the intangible qualities that separate truly exceptional interfaith leaders from merely good ones.

The conclusion summarizes the main themes of the book in the context of a concrete example.

Interfaith work is often referred to as "bridge building." My favorite bridge is a literary one, from Italo Calvino's beautiful book *Invisible Cities*. In one chapter, the traveler Marco Polo describes to the emperor Kublai Khan a particular bridge in his kingdom. The emperor grows impatient and asks Polo to get to the point. He wants to know about the stone that holds the bridge together.

> The bridge is not held together by a stone, says Polo, it is held together by an arch.
> So tell me about the arch, says the Emperor.
> Without stones, retorts the traveler, there is no arch.[15]

Polo's bridge is the guiding metaphor for this book. As you read through, I hope you come to view yourself as a bridge builder (identity), develop an understanding of the complex landscape you are building on (theory), get a clear image of the destination you are building toward (vision), acquire the stones that are the main materials of the bridge (knowledge base), build the aptitude to connect the stones into an arch strong enough to hold a diverse community (skill set), and cultivate the intangibles that give people enough confidence in your leadership to risk the journey (qualities).

IDENTITY

Bridges don't fall from the sky or rise from the ground. People build them. Becoming the kind of person who sees her identity linked to building interfaith bridges starts not with knowledge or skills, but with exploring your own story and narrating your identity.

ONE

The Identity of
an Interfaith Leader

In December 1995, when I was a senior at the University of Illinois, a professor handed me a copy of the *Atlantic Monthly* and suggested I read the article about Muhammad Yunus. Titled "The Barefoot Bank with Cheek," and written by journalist David Bornstein, it chronicled Yunus's journey from a PhD in economics at Vanderbilt University in Nashville to founding the Grameen Bank in Bangladesh.[1] Yunus had returned to his homeland to take up an academic post and found himself a witness to the terrible famine of 1974 that took as many as 1.5 million lives in his country. He began to be seriously concerned about poverty and started going to local villages to run social programs and ask searching questions. On a trip to the village of Jobra, he met a woman named Sufiya Khatun.

Sufiya was a widow trying to support herself and her children by weaving bamboo stools. She made two cents a day for her work. That number must be wrong, Yunus thought to himself. The price of a bamboo stool in the market was far higher than that, and the cost of the raw materials was quite low; the profit margin had to be larger than two cents. Sufiya explained to him that the only way a poor village widow could get the raw materials to make a bamboo stool, or any craft bought in the market, was through an unscrupulous middleman. The prices middlemen charged for raw materials were so unfairly high that the earnings of people like her wound up being unfathomably small.

Yunus canvassed the village and discovered forty-two others in Sufiya's position, mostly women, many of them widows. They worked hard, creating beautiful crafts that well-to-do people happily bought in the market, but their earnings were meager because of unfair labor and lending practices. Yunus calculated how much money it would take to help these forty-two villagers buy raw materials directly. The total amount was about twenty-six dollars. At that point, Yunus made a crucial decision. He reached into his own pocket to give the money, but he made it a loan, not a gift. The women would have to repay it, and they were responsible for the loan as a collective, not as forty-two separate individuals.

The women thrived, Yunus got his loan repaid, and it set him to thinking about all the people in Bangladesh who were in Sufiya's position. There must be millions of them, hardworking people who were honest and skilled but had no ability to buy raw materials directly because they lacked the capital and had no access to credit. Obviously, they couldn't all come to him for a loan. But there was an institution whose purpose it was to give loans to people who were starting businesses: a bank. Yunus went to see a banker friend to test out his interest in a loan program that would focus on industrious women in villages. His friend at the bank received the idea with a dismissive laugh.

Yunus was not to be dissuaded. The problem of unfair labor and lending practices in Bangladeshi villages was deep and widespread, but the prospect of giving microloans to skilled women to start their own small businesses held great promise. If traditional banks did not want to take this on, Yunus would do it himself. And so began the Grameen Bank, and the field of microfinance.

"The thing that strikes me about this guy," I said as I handed the magazine back to my professor, "is that he didn't just write a book about the issue or start a series of demonstrations against the government or the banks. He actually built the solution."

My professor nodded and said, "Muhammad Yunus is what's called a 'social entrepreneur,' somebody who designs and implements real-world solutions to real-world social problems. The guy who invented the term is named Bill Drayton. He's got an organization called Ashoka that finds social entrepreneurs around the world and gives them money to develop and spread their ideas."

That article, and my conversation with my professor, changed my life. Growing up in the western suburbs of Chicago in the early 1990s, I believed that there were basically four career paths in the world—lawyer, doctor, accountant, and engineer. That's what the successful parents seemed to be, and that's what the smart kids in my graduating class wanted to become. In college, my world opened up a little. I met people who were heading off to graduate school to become professors, and a handful who wanted to be writers of some sort. As a geeky sociology major who loved pontificating about the intersection of theory and practice, I began to think in those directions.

But, in my heart, I'd always been a kid who created things. It began when I was in high school. The course offerings in the social studies department felt a little stale to me. Moreover, I always wondered why history and literature were taught separately when there were such obvious connections between the two. Poking around in the school library, I discovered a section that wove these disciplines together. Called "humanities," it made me think that a class integrating those perspectives would be a lot more interesting than what was currently on the books. I asked the chair of the social studies department at Glenbard South High School if he would teach the course; he said fine, if the principal approved, and I got enough students to register. I set to work enrolling my friends and convincing the principal to sign off. I loved every minute of the process. I may have enjoyed the organizing more than the actual class.

And that's just one example. Growing up, I volunteered through the B. R. Ryall YMCA in Glen Ellyn, but I always wanted to start new service projects rather than simply plug into the existing options. When

I got to the University of Illinois and started volunteering in local shelters and soup kitchens, the pattern continued. What's more, I began to connect the academic work I was doing in classes to the programs I was designing. If it was true that most people got jobs through social networks and connections, as my sociology professors taught, then perhaps ladling soup wasn't the most effective thing for college students to be doing with their volunteer hours. Maybe we should help the unemployed homeless folks at the shelters build the social connections that would help them find jobs. So instead of organizing volunteers to staff food service at shelters, I started to create programs that focused on expanding the networks of people in local shelters.

Was I naïve? Without a doubt. But the rudiments of a particular imagination were at work. I probably spent as many hours analyzing social problems and designing new programs to address them as I did studying for classes in college. I remember thinking to myself, "Boy, I'm going to miss these days." I figured once I graduated I'd have to enter the real world—law school, probably, or graduate school in sociology, if I could convince my parents that the professor track was a viable option. From there on out, it would be all nose to the grindstone, no time for walking the streets and wondering what cool program I might cook up to improve the elementary school here or brighten up the vacant lot over there.

Then I got handed that Bornstein article and had that conversation with Professor Howie Schein. I was fascinated by Muhammad Yunus's work and the Grameen Bank, but the thing that struck me most deeply was the term Professor Schein had used to describe Yunus: "social entrepreneur," somebody who analyzed problems in the social world and shaped programs to solve them. Yunus had gotten to the heart of a social problem (poverty as a result of unfair labor and lending practices), created an elegant and innovative solution (microcredit given to collectives of women), and built an institution (the Grameen Bank) that spread the solution all over Bangladesh and, as the years progressed, the world. What's more, he headed Grameen and got paid a salary for it. Maybe lawyer-doctor-engineer-accountant-professor weren't the only available lives. Maybe I wouldn't have to stop analyzing social problems and designing neat programs to address them when I graduated from college. Maybe social entrepreneur could be a vocation and a career.

For weeks on end, "social entrepreneur" felt to me like the two most beautiful words in the English language (I told you I was a nerd). I spent hours reading up on Ashoka and Bill Drayton. I started to view the founders of the coolest organizations of the early 1990s—Wendy Kopp of Teach for America, Michael Brown and Alan Khazei of City Year, Vanessa Kirsch of Public Allies—not as social activists or social service providers but as social entrepreneurs. They had identified and analyzed a set of problems, shaped solutions, and built effective organizations to implement and scale those solutions.

I was experiencing the power of a clearly articulated identity category. When people asked what I did, or the kind of work I was interested in pursuing after college, saying, "Well, I'm a guy who likes to design and implement cool projects that help people by solving social problems" was going to be met with a cross-eyed stare. Saying I was a "social entrepreneur" sounded a lot crisper.

But the most important thing that the identity category "social entrepreneur" did for me wasn't about what I told people at parties; it was about how I understood my own identity, how I shaped my personal focus and growth. I started to join networks of others who called themselves social entrepreneurs, studied the thought leaders and exemplars of the movement, read the literature, and attempted to embody the best practices. I learned quickly that what I had done in the past—starting that humanities class in high school or the new programs I designed for homeless shelters—was only the first part of social entrepreneurship. Yes, I had identified an undesirable situation, used both creativity and research to design a solution, and implemented the new project. But I had no idea whether the new project actually worked. Did any of those homeless folks in Champaign-Urbana actually get jobs through the programs I designed? Nor had I given any thought to how I might build an institution that would spread the program elsewhere. If I was going to call myself a social entrepreneur, I quickly learned from the circles I was running in and the literature I was reading, I was going to have to do all of those things.

In my last year in college, as I saw myself more and more as a social entrepreneur, I was also starting to get more interested in religion. Growing up, I'd viewed religion as irrelevant, something my mom made me do every so often. But a variety of things converged to make me look at religion differently in my college years. As I said earlier, I was heavily involved in both service and social justice work in college, and that led me to Dorothy Day and the radical social movement that she founded, the Catholic Worker. The St. Jude Catholic Worker House of Hospitality was one of the local homeless shelters in my college town, but when I volunteered there, it felt qualitatively different from the Salvation Army or the Men's Emergency Shelter or any of the other agencies where I spent time. There was no staff-client distinction at St. Jude, and there was a lot more joy. It was a community, not an agency. When I inquired about how that came to be, the Catholic Workers told me to read the work of Dorothy Day. I found her writing luminous, particularly because it cut through the noise of theory and analysis with a simple and beautiful philosophy: poverty and war were not only unjust, they were against the will of God. It ought to be our purpose to end both. Living in community with those on the margins was what God wanted of us, Jesus showed us how to do it best, and following that path was the most fulfilling life possible. Day had walked it herself for fifty years.

I wanted Day's sense of purpose and strength of conviction. In both her writing and her life, she seemed to say, "If you want this, go to the source: God."

My admiration for Day and the Catholic Worker movement helped me see religion through new eyes. It occurred to me that many of my heroes—Martin Luther King Jr., Mahatma Gandhi, Malcolm X, Mother Teresa, Archbishop Desmond Tutu, His Holiness the Dalai Lama—were people of deep faith, people whose religions played a central role in the work they did. What's more, they were from different religious communities. Day was Catholic; King, a Baptist; Tutu, an Episcopalian; Gandhi, a Hindu; Malcolm, a Muslim; and the Dalai Lama, a Buddhist. Something about how these people connected with their respective traditions had given them great courage and power. How could I ever have thought religion was irrelevant?

At the same time, I was getting a clearer picture of the dark side of the relevance of religion in the world. As an undergraduate, I was deeply involved in the campus diversity movement and enjoyed nothing more than lecturing my father about what I liked to call "people of color consciousness." Generally speaking, he received these lectures with good humor, figuring, I suppose, that it was part of the cost of sending his son to college. But, at some point, I must have crossed a line and he got frustrated and said, "Listen, the next time you want to lecture me about diversity, why don't you tell me how you are going to solve the most important identity challenge in the world: conflicts over religion."

The following week, my girlfriend at the time called me and, choking back tears, said, "Yitzhak Rabin has just been assassinated." My girlfriend was Jewish and regarded Rabin as one of the great faith heroes of the twentieth century, the man who would lead Israel and the Jews to peace with the Palestinians. She was utterly heartbroken over the assassination, and what was left of her heart after the murder was shattered by the fact that the killer was Jewish and claimed that his accomplice in the assassination was God. For me, it was a wake-up call to the ugly role that religion was playing in world affairs. Protestant-Catholic conflict in Northern Ireland, Hindu-Muslim conflict in India, Christian-Muslim conflict in the Balkans, Buddhist-Hindu conflict in Sri Lanka, and, of course, the granddaddy of them all, the Jewish-Muslim conflict in the Middle East. Why hadn't I noticed the religious dimension of global affairs before? And why was religion never part of the diversity discussion in college?

Add to this another insight. The foot soldiers of religious extremism always seemed to be young. Yigal Amir, the man who murdered Prime Minister Rabin, was twenty-six at the time. But my faith heroes had begun their journeys when they were young as well. Martin Luther King Jr. was the same age as Yigal Amir when he led the Montgomery bus boycott. The Dalai Lama and Mahatma Gandhi were even younger when they began their movements. What's more, all of my faith heroes seemed to have an intense experience with another faith during their formative years. Gandhi read the Bible as a young man in law school, and King read Gandhi as a young man in seminary.

In the summer of 1998, I was lucky enough to be at the United Religions Initiative Global Summit at Stanford University and meet a group of like-minded young people from around the world. We talked excitedly about the prospect of creating programs that brought together young people who were oriented around religion differently to do service projects and engage in conversations about how their various faiths inspired them to serve. It would increase the amount of service being done in the world, strengthen relationships between diverse communities, enhance the leadership of young people, and raise the volume on faith as a positive rather than a destructive force. Organizations like Teach for America, City Year, and Public Allies were intentional about bringing people of different racial, ethnic, and class backgrounds together around service, but they didn't touch faith. The project we envisioned would employ the same basic approach of using service as a common table to gather diversity, but the dimension of identity we would emphasize was faith.

A small group of us launched an initiative called Interfaith Youth Corps and started running interfaith service-learning projects with young people in different parts of the world. After defining a methodology that seemed to work across a range of settings—and changing the "Corps" part of our name to "Core" to reflect our vision of being at the heart of a larger movement—we started to build the foundation of an organization that could improve and scale our program. In addition to continuing to organize interfaith service projects, we began to write and speak about interfaith service learning, hold conferences for colleagues in the growing movement, and design a curriculum for the emerging field.

A few years after the article on Muhammad Yunus, David Bornstein wrote another piece for the same magazine on Bill Drayton, the founder of Ashoka, and the field of social entrepreneurship.[2] In that article,

Bornstein profiled Ashoka fellow Fábio Rosa, who designed and spread an innovation that brought electricity to tens of millions of poor people in Brazil. When Bornstein asked him about what the Ashoka Fellowship meant to him, Rosa responded, "Bill [Drayton] made me see that I was a social entrepreneur. He showed me that my role was to take things beyond theory and find practical solutions for all the problems along the way."[3] In 2004, when I was awarded an Ashoka Fellowship for founding Interfaith Youth Core (IFYC), I said much the same thing to Drayton. He had created the identity category that I aspired to be part of, and now I was being ushered into the inner circle. It was one of the proudest moments of my life.

Meanwhile, IFYC kept on running interfaith service-learning programs and trying to grow the field. I found myself on the road more and more, speaking especially at college campuses. After a talk I gave about IFYC at Nazareth College in Rochester, New York, a young woman approached me and said, "Your organization has inspired me to be an interfaith leader." Up until that point, "interfaith leader" was a term I had used offhandedly. But that woman's comment made me realize that "interfaith leader" could be an identity category like "social entrepreneur." All of the benefits of aspiring to be part of an identity category came flooding back to me. This is a big part of IFYC's contribution, I realized, and we have to start doing it more deliberately.

That is why I have devoted an entire chapter to "interfaith leader" as an identity category. My purpose here is to encourage you to internalize "interfaith leader" as an identity, just as others have adopted "human rights activist," "environmentalist," or "civil rights worker" (you can be more than one, by the way). When something becomes part of your identity, you commit to it for the long haul, you begin to see the world through that lens, and you seek to constantly improve your knowledge base, skill set, and craft. It becomes a way of being in the world.

So what does it mean to identify as an interfaith leader? In *True North*, Harvard Business School professor Bill George argues that the distinguishing quality of effective leaders is authenticity and that authentic leadership emerges most profoundly from your life story. George defines authenticity as the intersection of passion and purpose, and says it can only truly be achieved by taking a long, hard look at one's own experiences, discerning the path they point toward, and following that path to its logical conclusion. He writes, "Leaders are defined by their unique life stories and the way they frame their stories to discover their passions and the purpose of their leadership."[4] This is especially relevant for interfaith leaders because most of us get started in this work for very personal reasons.

George's technique of locating identity in life stories follows in the tradition of Paul Ricoeur, one of the most important philosophers of modern times. Ricoeur developed a theory called "narrative identity," which states that we understand who we are by the stories we tell to ourselves about ourselves. Ricoeur illustrates by asking people to imagine pictures of themselves across their lifetime.[5] The physical differences between your baby picture and the image of you now are immense. If you showed a stranger the pictures of yourself at very different life stages, she may not guess that the images are of the same person.

How do you connect such radically different pictures of yourself and understand them as representing a single entity, namely you? The answer, Ricoeur asserts, is by creating a plot out of the events of your life. Simply put, by telling stories *about* your self *to* your self. We do this on a regular basis, by journaling or processing the day aloud with friends and family. We also do this over time, by telling stories that start with lines like "I like grape popsicles because when I was a kid my mom used to give them to me on hot summer nights after a long day of playing outside." To Ricoeur, this common human practice of highlighting events in our lives and establishing causal links between them are the way we form our identity.

A final thing to say about Ricoeur's understanding of narrative identity: key moments in our lives almost always involve other people. Our lives, and our stories about our lives, are like narrative threads that cross, connect, and interweave with the narrative threads of the lives of others. This idea is particularly important for the identities of interfaith leaders precisely because interfaith leadership is by definition about how we interact with other people.

What about your life story would help you identify as an interfaith leader? The remainder of this chapter presents a simple structure for highlighting and connecting life experiences in a manner that adds up to seeing yourself as an interfaith leader. I will illustrate the various "moments" by telling how the stories of other interfaith leaders influenced their vocation. I hope that by telling their stories, you will be able to locate, interpret, and narrate the moments in your life that form your own interfaith leadership identity story.

Here are five types of personal experiences that I think are important to reflect upon and narrate to yourself as you consider the identity category "interfaith leader."

- Moments of inspiration or enrichment from people or ideas of other traditions
- Moments of connection or relationship with people or ideas of other traditions
- Moments of prejudice or conflict with people or ideas of other traditions
- Moments of action or cooperation with people or ideas of other traditions
- Moments of recognizing difference with other religious people or ideas, yet feeling admiration

Earlier in this chapter, in my brief outline of my own path to interfaith leadership, just about all of the elements of this framework are present. There are moments of inspiration (reading about Dorothy Day), moments of cooperation (volunteering at the Catholic Worker), moments when I recognized the scourge of religious violence (the murder of Yitzhak Rabin), and moments when I connected with someone from another tradition (sympathy with the deep sadness my Jewish friend felt at Rabin's assassination). *Acts of Faith*, my first book, is a longer, more developed story of my personal journey to interfaith leadership. As I read that book now, it is clear to me that I was intuitively writing in the narrative structure I outline here, although I did not know it at the time.

Not all interfaith leadership narratives have all the components I articulate later. Nor are the various categories necessarily mutually exclusive. For example, you can have your moment of inspiration with someone from a different religion while you are cooperating with him. Moreover, I don't think there is a particular order in which these five things have to happen. But I do believe that most interfaith leaders will have a deep sense of when at least some of these moments occurred, and how those experiences shaped their identities as interfaith leaders. In a later chapter, I write about the key skill of using such moments to form a public narrative that can inspire others to begin thinking of themselves as interfaith leaders.

Moments of inspiration or enrichment from people or ideas of other traditions

When Judith Berling first heard about the Daoist fire-walking ceremony, she figured she should go, although her hopes were not especially high. It was 1971 and she was a graduate student in Taiwan studying Chinese religious life and practice. Everything was fieldwork, including, she supposed, something as kitschy as a fire-walking ceremony. She had no idea that the evening would shape her vocation as a scholar of Chinese religions and her faith life as a Christian.

By the time she arrived at the temple, the entire area around the charcoal coals was burning with such intensity that she immediately had to make her way to the opposite side of the courtyard. She was surprised to discover that the participants were not Daoist masters showing off, but young apprentices seeking to pass an early test on their path to the priesthood. She watched them gathered in the corner, barefoot and chanting Daoist scriptures meant to invoke protective spirits. In the center of the room was the fire, a full eighteen inches high. Judith could barely bring herself to watch as each young acolyte, carrying a statue of a deity, circumambulated the flame and then ran over the hot coals three times, chanting mantras throughout.

After the process, each priest-in-training was brought before the Daoist master, who examined their feet and legs for burns. Acolytes who were unscathed had been successful in their invocation of the Daoist gods of protection, passing the test. At least this was what Judith gathered. There was no Daoist host, explainer, or interpreter. Judith had to process the experience on her own.

Witnessing this ritual unmoored Judith, both as a scholar and as a Christian. She did not "believe" in either the Daoist spirits or the idea of fire walking as a valid test for religious leadership. Yet she had seen these young men calmly run through the fire and come out without burns. And even though she had neither rational explanation nor even a relevant frame of reference for what she just witnessed, she recognized that some kind of spiritual elevation had taken place.

When she returned to the United States and attended a Christian church for worship, Judith discovered that the old familiar ritual of hearing scripture read aloud and then coolly interpreted by the pastor was no longer spiritually resonant for her. Her experience of Daoism had made the dimension of God that is an unknowable mystery paramount in her faith life. But most American Christian churches she knew of sought to explain the divine and, thus, felt too neat and contained.

One day, Judith attended the Great Vigil of Easter at an Episcopal parish. The service relied on dynamic symbols (light and darkness, chanting and music) rather than verbal explanations to dramatize the biblical story. As Judith sat through the epic—from creation to the flood to the birth, death, and resurrection of Christ—it struck a place deep inside her that had been unmoved for a long time. Judith felt herself coming back to Christian worship and the church, grateful to have encountered modes in her home faith that helped her explore the ineffable dimensions of the divine. She writes, "The fire walking opened up for me a new dimension of religious sensibility that has greatly enriched my life both as a scholar and as a person of faith . . . it has also made me more open to many dimensions of my own tradition and even—dare I say—of my relationship to God."[6]

Moments of connection or relationship with people
or ideas of other traditions

Josh Stanton's choice to become a rabbi came as a result of a connection with someone who was not Jewish.

Josh remembers his student days at Amherst as a constant swirl of classes and extracurricular activities. Most were interesting enough, but none captured his heart or offered him a calling. He felt most alive during Shabbat services on Friday nights. He would arrive early to set up and prepare the dinner, and stay late to help clean up. "On Shabbat, my joy seemed to overflow," he recalls.

He was not the only one to notice. One Friday night, Paul Sorrentino ambled up to Josh and said, "Have you ever considered becoming a rabbi?"

The question, although simple and obvious enough considering Josh's weekly leadership at Shabbat, took him by surprise. Students went to Amherst to become bankers and consultants, not rabbis. But over time, through many conversations with Paul, Josh began to discern a call to the rabbinate. He went to a Jewish seminary after he graduated from Amherst and was ordained in the summer of 2013.

What makes this story striking is that Paul Sorrentino is not a professor of Jewish history or even a fellow student who participated in Shabbat services. He was an evangelical pastor—the Reverend Paul Sorrentino—who simply paid attention to the joy and fulfillment Josh exhibited when he came to the Center for Religious Life at Amherst on Friday nights to prepare for Shabbat. In his senior sermon, Josh credits his relationship with this evangelical pastor for mentoring him into his vocation as a rabbi.

Moments of prejudice or conflict with people
or ideas of other traditions

Mary Ellen Giess grew up in a Unitarian Universalist family outside Philadelphia and attended the University of North Carolina. When she arrived in Chapel Hill, she was surprised by the outsized role evangelical Christianity played in public life. Preachers holding signs condemning all non-Christians to hell and student groups handing out Bibles were common sights around town. Mary Ellen was put off by these groups, even a little intimidated. Every time she passed someone handing out Bibles or shouting Christian slogans, she felt belittled and judged.

She was happy to come across a small Unitarian group on campus, finding that those students shared her experience of feeling on the margins of campus religious life. The group also provided an opportunity to express many of her deeply held commitments, including frequent social action projects in the local community. After its weekly worship meeting, the group would often gather on the UNC quad where a Hare Krishna group served a delicious vegetarian supper.

On one of these evenings, as Mary Ellen was hanging out with her Unitarian friends, the conversation shifted to their disagreements with what they considered judgmental religious groups. From there, the talk turned to their distaste for conservative religion more generally and then, somehow, to Mormons in particular. Mary Ellen found herself laughing along as her friends made fun of the conservative sexual mores of Mormons and their "magic underwear."

Their laughter was interrupted by a young woman who had been sitting nearby and had gotten up to angrily confront Mary Ellen and her friends. She said, "I've been listening to you make fun of my religion for the last fifteen minutes, and I just wanted to let you know that I'm a Mormon and I'm proud of it. I'm actually wearing what you derisively call 'magic underwear.' You can think it's a joke, but I believe it is a connection to holiness." The young woman walked away, pushing a stroller with her baby inside.

Mary Ellen is a senior member of IFYC's staff and a close friend of mine. Her eyes well with tears when she recounts this story, both because of the hurt it caused the Mormon woman and because her actions violated the core beliefs of her Unitarian Universalist tradition—justice, equity, and compassion in human relations.

Moments of action or cooperation with people or ideas of other traditions

Ibrahim Abdul-Matin decided that he needed to expand his horizons and test his will. As he had never been out of the northeast, he figured a twenty-two-day Outward Bound trip in Joshua Tree National Park would do the trick. After an arduous journey getting to a Wild West desert town called Twentynine Palms, Ibrahim was excited to meet his fellow travelers. All of them seemed friendly except one, Christian, who immediately informed the group that the end of the world was near and whoever did not accept Jesus Christ as Lord and Savior better get ready to burn in hell. Muslims, he explained, would burn in the hottest part.

Ibrahim is a Muslim. He is also a pretty big guy. So was Christian. As there were no naturally occurring water sources on the trail (the group hiked from water cache to water cache), the two biggest people in the group were automatically tasked to be the water carriers. Ibrahim and Christian were destined to spend a lot of time together.

The first few days were bristly, but slowly the common task of carrying water helped them form a bond. They discovered that it was more pleasant to talk to one another while carrying the large jugs of water than walk in stubborn silence. When Ibrahim woke early to make *fajr* prayer, he was surprised to see Christian already awake, praying. In their conversations, they were struck by the fact that they were both processing the physical experience through their respective religious frameworks. They made clear that they disagreed with the other's doctrine, but still found ways to support the other's faith. For example, if one did not wake in time for early morning prayers, the other would nudge him.

For the final leg of an Outward Bound trip, the instructor separates and the group members have to choose two navigators. They chose Christian and Ibrahim, two people who disagreed on doctrine and still managed to build a friendship, support one another's faith, and could be trusted to lead the group home.

MOMENTS OF RECOGNIZING DIFFERENCE WITH OTHER RELIGIOUS PEOPLE OR IDEAS, YET FEELING ADMIRATION

Walter Kirn found himself disgusted by the anti-Mormon prejudice being aired by much of the mainstream media during Mitt Romney's presidential run in 2012. He was especially upset by people who fancied themselves educated and progressive. For example, Charles Blow, a columnist for the *New York Times*, made a derisive reference to the ritual clothing some Mormons wear, calling it "magic underwear."

Walter responded by writing an essay for the *New Republic* about his little-known past as a Mormon, his break with the doctrine of the Church of Jesus Christ of Latter-day Saints (LDS), and his continued admiration for the community. He begins the essay by recounting difficult stories from his childhood. His father was teetering on the edge of insanity—talking to himself in public, letting his legal business shrivel and die—and Walter's whole world seemed on the brink of falling apart. On a flight home, in a particularly deep despair, Walter's father found himself seated next to a Mormon couple "that radiated serenity and calm." He shared his story with them, and they helped make sure he got where he was going safely. They also got the church involved in his life. Mormons started to show up at the Kirn household, offering friendship and support. Grateful for the stability and community, the Kirns became Mormons.

Walter left the church in his late teens. He had stopped believing in LDS doctrine, no longer felt moved by Mormon rituals and ceremonies, and frequently violated the church's restrictions on sexuality. When he turned seventeen, he decided not to serve a Mormon mission, as the vast majority of LDS boys do.

Yet he continued to appreciate the Mormon commitment to community. It had served Walter well in his childhood, and it turned out he needed it in adulthood as well. In the article, Walter recalls a time when he felt his own life spiraling downward. He was recently divorced, taking too many meds, and on the brink of financial ruin. He traveled to Los Angeles to pursue a new relationship and some creative projects, and needed a place to stay. His poor credit score got him bounced from several guesthouses, but one landlord seemed willing to take a chance on him. Turns out, the landlord was Mormon. A number of people in the little housing development were Mormon as well. Not only did they let Walter borrow old sofas and tables for his apartment, they cleaned the furniture first and helped move it inside his apartment.

He hung out with the Mormon crew during their barbecues and ice cream socials. He was invited to attend weddings and to ride along on road trips. Nobody said anything judgmental when it was clear that Walter's girlfriend was spending the night at his place, and nobody pressured him to attend worship services. He was allowed to be part of the community in the ways that were comfortable for him.

In that space, Walter's life began to feel full and balanced again. He writes, "I'd forgotten that social life could be so easy. I'd forgotten that things most Americans do alone, ordinary things, like watching television or listening to music or sweeping a floor, could also be done in numbers, pleasantly . . . the direction of the pursuit of happiness was toward the advancement of the common good."[7]

Walter's life is an excellent illustration of how you can have both profound disagreements with some dimensions of a religion and still appreciate, even gain from, other parts of it.

The Muslim poet Rumi says that there are many ways we can tell our stories, as romances, dirty jokes, or righteous struggles. I love that line because it reminds me that our lives are made up of countless moments and open to myriad interpretations. A narrative identity is not a laundry list of random personal happenings. It is a careful selection and stringing together of the moments and events that matter for a particular purpose. In other words, one's narrative identity is an act of intentional interpretation and meaning making. You choose the events that matter, you choose how to string them together, and you choose how they inform the path you walk now. Your identity is not handed to you. It is a product of the life events you emphasize and how you connect those events.

Each of the people I've highlighted illustrates how narrating an early interfaith "moment" helps to develop an identity that guides your future actions. Walter Kirn continues to write about faith and life in a manner that respectfully marks disagreement and also highlights resonances. After her experience with the Daoist fire-walking ceremony, Judith Berling further committed to her academic path, becoming a well-regarded professor of Chinese religions and a highly respected public voice on what Christians can learn from other traditions. Josh

Stanton's experience with Reverend Paul Sorrentino at Amherst moved him to be a rabbi who is highly attuned to the well-being of people in other traditions, speaking out forcefully against religious prejudice. Ibrahim Abdul-Matin's time with Christian in the Outward Bound program inspired a lifetime of interfaith environmental activism grounded in his Muslim faith, beautifully captured in his book *Green Deen*. Mary Ellen Giess's experience made her vow to stand up to religious prejudice and led her to Interfaith Youth Core, where she is our senior director for cocurricular programs.

Highlighting, connecting, and narrating interfaith experiences from your past can help you develop an interfaith leadership identity that guides your future.

I want to close this chapter by highlighting a final dimension of Paul Ricoeur's concept of narrative identity as connected to interfaith leadership. Recall that Ricoeur highlighted the key role that interactions with others, and the stories we tell about them, play in the formation of our identities. There is another role that the presence of others plays: they remind us that we are responsible to people beyond ourselves. The promises we make to other people, both overt and implicit, are central to Ricoeur's ethics of identity. People want to know of their friends and families, followers want to know of their leaders, "Where are you?" By narrating our life story in a particular way, Ricoeur says, we are announcing to people who count on us: "Here I am."

In other words, we do not just tell stories about such moments in our lives to ourselves; we also tell these stories to other people. As we do that, we begin to make promises to the world about who we are and what we can do. We are saying, implicitly at least, "You can count on us to help people who orient around religion differently get along more positively." We are saying to a world that desperately needs interfaith leaders: Here we are.

THEORY

These next two chapters break the term "interfaith" into two parts. The "inter" in interfaith stands for interaction between people who orient around religion differently. The "faith" in interfaith stands for how people relate to their religious and ethical traditions. Put together, "interfaith" is about how our interactions with those who are different have an impact on the way we relate to our religious and ethical traditions, and how our relationships with our traditions have an impact on our interactions with those who are different from us.

I prefer the term "interfaith" to other commonly used terms, namely, multifaith and interreligious. I prefer "inter" to "multi" because the world has long been "multi" in the sense that people who orient around religion differently have existed on the same planet at the same time. Our era is distinct in the interaction between diverse individuals and groups. I prefer "faith" to "religious" because interfaith leaders are not primarily concerned with abstract religious systems (for example, Hinduism or Judaism) interacting; we are concerned with real-world people who relate to these religious traditions coming into contact with one another.

In the metaphor that governs this book, these chapters describe the landscape on which interfaith leaders build their bridges.

TWO

The "Inter" in Interfaith

"Modernity pluralizes," writes the renowned social theorist Peter Berger.[1] For the vast majority of human history, the vast majority of humankind lived the vast majority of their lives in a world of people who were largely similar to them. The distinguishing feature of our age (dating from the middle of the twentieth century) is pluralization, meaning the frequent and intense interaction between people with different identities. Technological advances in air travel and communications, increased migration coupled with the growth of global cities, and the end of colonialism and the decline of both legal and social barriers between different groups have all led to a world where contact between diverse people and ideas is simply standard operating procedure. As Robert Putnam puts it in his paper "*E Pluribus Unum*: Diversity and Community in the 21st Century": "The most certain prediction that we can make about almost any modern society is that it will be more diverse a generation from now than it is today."[2]

I look will at the impact of pluralization at four levels:

- Individual identity
- Continuity of religious communities
- Microenvironments
- Macroenvironments

To bring social theory to life, I will provide a sketch of an American town with a predominantly Methodist population that starts to experience diversity when a Muslim family moves in. I will ask you to put yourself in the position of various characters at the four levels I've mentioned, and see the world from their perspective. All of the characters are composites of people that I know. They are meant to provide insights into how people in their various complexities respond to diversity, rather than serve as stereotypes. Of course, for everyone I know who acts like one of the characters I've sketched below, I know ten others with the same identity characteristics (Methodist teenager, Pakistani imam) who act differently.

INDIVIDUAL IDENTITY

The first character I'd like you to take the perspective of is a white, male Methodist teenager in a largely homogenous town. Your family has been Methodist for generations and you live in a neighborhood where seemingly everybody goes to a Methodist church on Sunday. You've never really wondered too much about being Methodist. It's simply the water you swim in, the way of the world.

One fine day, a Muslim family moves in down the street. You notice that they don't show up to church on Sundays. Someone mentions to you that the Muslim family takes Friday afternoons off for something called *jumma*. As you get ready for church one Sunday morning, you wonder what the teenagers in the Muslim family are doing at that time. As you imagine them sleeping in, you think to yourself, "If they aren't going to church, why am I going?" This is a question that literally never occurred to you before. Going to church on Sundays was simply automatic, like the sun rising. Sunday mornings existed for going to church. It is only the presence of people who do things differently that makes you reflect on your own patterns.

One of the teenagers from the Muslim family goes to your school. You've played pickup basketball games with him, and he sits at a nearby table for lunch. For a week now, he hasn't been at the basketball courts after school, and you haven't seen him in the cafeteria. As you come out of the lunchroom one day, you bump into him leaving the library. "How come you haven't been playing ball lately?" you ask. "It's Ramadan," he says. "I'm fasting all day. No food, no water." That explains why he hasn't been in the cafeteria either.

You Google "Ramadan" on your iPhone and read that it's one of the five pillars of Islam and lasts a month. No eating or drinking all day for a full month! Does that include weekends? Are you allowed to take a day off if you get sick?

You mention to your mother that a kid you play basketball with is Muslim and is fasting for Ramadan. He spends lunchtime in the library. She says, "You ought to eat your lunch quickly and go keep him company."

Your older brother walks down the stairs. He's overheard the conversation and adds his two cents: "Why would you do anything to help a Muslim? I say stay as far away from those people as you can."

So, what should you do? Keep the Muslim kid company or stay away?

As you are thinking this over, you overhear your mother arguing with your brother. "That's not a very Christian thing to say," your mother scolds. "We Christians are meant to be good neighbors. Jesus reached out to everyone. He was inclusive."

Your brother scoffs. "Muslims deny the Lordship of our savior Jesus Christ," he says. "They preach a false doctrine. Plus, you never know which one might turn out to be a terrorist. Why should we be good neighbors to them?"

This argument just adds another layer of complexity to your inner struggles. Five minutes ago, you were thinking to yourself, "Muslim dude is a pretty good ballplayer, and this Ramadan thing is fascinating. Sure, I'll go sit with him a few times over the next couple of weeks." But now your Christian identity is involved. Are Christians supposed to be good neighbors to people who don't believe in Jesus as Lord and Savior as your mother believes, or shun them as your brother says? Come to think of it, you've heard that "Lord and Savior" phrase repeated every Sunday at church since you can remember. But now, in the light of realizing somebody else doesn't believe it, you are wondering whether you really believe it yourself. If you decide that you don't believe it, do you have to go to church next Sunday?

Let's take a step back and see how social theory illuminates this sketch. The introduction of diversity into the life of the white, male Methodist teenager in the largely Methodist town has raised three questions: Who am I? Who are you? How do we relate to each other? When everybody around you is the same, you don't have to ask these questions. But once you come into contact with people who are different, those three questions begin to play in a loop in your mind. As the social theorist Anthony Giddens writes, "[In modernity] the self has become a *reflexive* project."[3]

Now let's consider this scenario from the perspective of the young Muslim. Imagine that you're him, and you've just moved into this town. In an area where just about everybody else goes to church on Sunday and doesn't seem to have any dietary restrictions, you are wondering why you have to fast for Ramadan and go to *jumma* prayers on Friday afternoons. When your parents came in to talk to the school principal about leaving school early on Friday, he was friendly, respectful, and accommodating. But your math teacher was different. He has mispronounced your name since the day you arrived, on purpose it seems, and was icy cold when you handed him the note from your parents, signed by the principal, about missing class on Fridays for prayers.

The whole thing made you feel uncomfortable, hyperaware of not only how you are different from others but how they are looking at you. Like everyone else, you hear the reports of Muslims being involved with terrorism, but you feel totally disconnected from those people, as if they are not even part of the same universe and certainly not the same religion. Yet, shockingly, other people put you in the same category with those murderers. A girl in your history class last week said her dad read a headline about a Muslim extremist group murdering Christians in the Middle East and said, "You know it's their religion that makes them that way. They're all like that."

Thank God for basketball. It's been a way of connecting with folks in this town. One of the guys who lives nearby and is a regular on the court asked you why you haven't been around lately. Mentioning Ramadan just kind of came out. Afterward, you wondered if you should have said something else, covered up what you were really doing. But he seemed cool about it. You've seen him and his family walk into the Methodist church on Sunday. You wonder if church is like *masjid*, and if Christian prayer is like Muslim prayer. When Ramadan is over and you go back to playing basketball in the afternoon, maybe you could ask that guy what goes on at church. In the back of your mind, though, you can't help but wonder if you are misreading the situation. What if your neighbor's curiosity about Ramadan is not a sign of kindness? What if he doesn't like Muslims, like your math teacher, or the girl's father who thinks all Muslims want to kill Christians?

One Friday, the imam who preaches at *jumma* pulls you close after prayers and warns you not to get too close to the Christians in this town. Their religion and culture is different, he says. You must stick close to your own values and practices. "What do they do in church?" you ask him.

"They never mention the Prophet Muhammad or the Qur'an and they say that Jesus is God," the imam responds sharply. "Associating any figure or object with God is *shirk*, unforgivable." You regret asking him the question.

You see the imam talking to your father outside. He is wagging his finger and saying that he is concerned you are getting too curious about Christians, maybe too close to them. He knows of a boarding school for young Muslims in America. Students there study math, science, and history, but also Qur'an and Hadith. They are taught the respect for Christians and Christianity that is rooted in the Qur'an, but they are not tempted by the presence of Christians to adopt their beliefs and practices.

Your father says to him sternly that the Prophet Muhammad was helped by many Christians in his mission. The family has felt welcomed by this community. They hope to build positive relationships with the Christians in this town by highlighting common ground. There are, for example, many Christian organizations here that serve the poor. He has been planning to bring his family to volunteer and highlight the shared Christian-Muslim value of helping those who are less fortunate.

The presence of diversity has set in motion a similar set of questions for both the young Muslim and the young Methodist, but they experience the intensity of those questions differently. There is a dramatic power difference between the two. The Methodist is part of the majority and gets to ask reflexive questions from the comfort of a world that understands his ways of being, believing, and belonging, where he has friends, where no one mispronounces his name. The young Muslim is in the minority and regards the young Methodist with some envy. It must be nice to be born into a world where you fit in. Not only is he as a Muslim different, his particular difference is viewed with suspicion. The "Who am I? Who are you? How do we relate to each other?" questions are common, but they are experienced in different ways depending on whether you are in the majority or in the minority.

CONTINUITY OF RELIGIOUS COMMUNITIES

Let's consider this situation from the position of the minister at the Methodist church. Members of your congregation have seemed restless lately. You've noticed that fewer teenagers are showing up on Sunday mornings. One father tells you that his son simply says, "Look, Dad, if you want to go to church, go. I'm just making a different choice." The father wants you to talk to his son. He is fuming and says, "Church as a choice? Who ever heard of that? God says you go to church—you go. That's what our family has done in this town for generations."

Modernity, writes Berger, poses a particular challenge to religious communities. The presence of alternative ways of being, believing, and belonging means that religious communities lose their "taken for granted" status.[4] Where it was once unthinkable to not attend church or be a Methodist in this town, the presence of people who do things differently makes other options viable. Religious communities in the situation of modernity become "voluntary associations," meaning that they need to compete for the attention of people who have a whole set of other options. Where once people understood their identity as fate, they now experience it as choice.

This shift is one of the most significant consequences of modernity. Here is how Jonathan Sacks, the former chief rabbi of Britain, explains it: "Long gone are the days when our identities, beliefs and life chances were narrowly circumscribed by where and to whom we happened to be born. We are no longer actors in a play written by tradition and directed by community, in which roles are allocated by accidents of birth. Instead, careers, relationships and lifestyles have become things we freely choose from a superstore of alternatives."[5]

As you listen to the father, you realize similar conversations are happening in homes all around this town. Some teenagers have stopped showing up at church altogether. Another group has taken to arriving early and sitting up front, wearing their Christian identities on their sleeves. The leader of that group approached you recently and asked you to point to the verses in the Bible that say Islam is wrong. You gently tell him that Islam emerged hundreds of years after the Bible was written, so it's not mentioned there at all. "But Islam is wrong, right?" the teenager blurts out.

The presence of the Muslim family seems to be inspiring all sorts of questions and causing all kinds of consternation. You are not exactly sure how to respond. Should you try to change things to make church more interesting for younger folks? If so, which group of younger folks—the ones who are no longer coming to church or the ones who are showing up early and demanding that you denounce Islam? Would changing things upset the older generation, like the father who spoke to you? Clearly, the way things are suits many of them. Also, how much should you talk about Islam and Muslims from the pulpit? You know the answer to this question is, "More." But your knowledge about the subject is pretty thin. The problem is, the people in the church who seem most comfortable talking about Islam and Muslims are the ones who know only negative things about the religion. You doubt they were all Islamic studies majors in college. More likely they are reading newsletters from organizations whose purpose is to spread ugliness about another religion and culture. All of this brings you to a big idea: you'll go see the imam who comes to town on Fridays to preach at Muslim services. Maybe you can get him to come to your church and do a guest presentation; that way, more of your congregation will meet a real, live Muslim. Furthermore, as a fellow religious leader, maybe he is experiencing some of the same generational challenges that you are. It will be fun to find out.

Let's switch characters again. I want you to imagine this conversation from the point of view of the imam, a recent immigrant from Pakistan who works professionally as an engineer and takes Fridays off to travel to various towns in the region giving *khutbas* (sermons at Muslim prayer gatherings).

You are surprised to receive a phone call from a woman who introduces herself as the minister of the local Methodist church and requests a meeting at the local coffee shop. When you arrive, she buys your coffee and is extremely friendly. She shakes your hand vigorously. Generally, you don't shake hands with women, but it seems very out of place to tell her that, so you nervously allow her to pump your hand up and down. You are hoping she doesn't try to hug you at some point. That you will not do. As she begins talking, you are plotting in your mind how to escape an attempted hug and not come across as rude.

She sips her coffee and talks about the challenges she is facing in her church. Some of the young people are saying they do not want to come anymore and others have taken a somewhat fundamentalist turn. The older generation is not happy about any of this. Much of the issue centers around the new Muslim family that has moved into the neighborhood. You know this family. You tried to talk some sense into the father just last week about how to ensure that his children follow the straight path of Islam instead of being tempted by Christianity and American culture. Instead of thanking you, the father basically told you to back off.

The Methodist minister keeps on saying that change is good; she welcomes it. She wants to have dialogues between the generations. She wants to have open discussions about Islam, especially about how Jesus is shared between the two religions. On the one hand, you appreciate that she seems to want to know positive things about Islam, but you are suspicious of her general attitude. In your view, the kind of changes she is talking about—young people rejecting religion, discord between parents and children—is not good. Open discussion is certainly not the solution to such problems. The solution is to reiterate loudly and clearly what the truth is and to tell people that, if they don't follow it, there will be dire consequences. This Jesus talk is also making you uncomfortable, especially as she seems to combine it with an invitation to attend her church. Is this her way of trying to convert you? She seems too nice to be engaging in a bait and switch, but some of your Muslim friends have said that Christians will do anything to convert Muslims. Maybe the fact that she is a woman is throwing you off. You are not used to meeting with women in this way, and a woman wearing a religious collar is especially new for you. You do a lot of nodding during the meeting. At the end, your fear comes true—she leans in to hug you. You back away, but she doesn't seem to notice. You feel her hands touching your shoulders. You sense that she does not mean to make you uncomfortable, but while walking back to your car, your feelings bounce between guilt, frustration, and anger. Why did you not stand up for your values and your religion during that meeting?

As you drive away, you are remembering a town hall meeting you attended a few months ago in a nearby city. A man stood up and introduced himself as a conservative Catholic. A few people in the crowd hissed, but the man stood tall and proud. He started off by saying that he saw changes happening in the town and he didn't like those changes. He didn't like that the school play had a kissing scene and that a youth club had an openly gay leader. He didn't like the new people moving in, with their strange un-Christian ways. At a local restaurant, he saw a teenage girl talk back to her father, and the dad just sat there and took it. He insisted that would never have happened when he was growing up. He wanted to say out loud to everyone that he knew of a Catholic academy a few miles away whose academic and extracurricular program was focused on Christian living. There was no kissing in school plays and no talking back to authority figures. He would be enrolling his children there in the fall. If anyone else in the crowd was interested, they could see him.

You cannot help but contrast what you heard from that man with the conversation you just had with the Methodist minister. The Methodist minister was open and friendly and seemed to want to learn about Islam, while the Catholic man was certainly implying that part of the change he didn't like was Muslims moving into the area. Still, you felt a sense of kinship with the Catholic man. Your general orientation and attitude are much closer to his than that of the Methodist minister. Like him, you don't like many of the changes you are seeing. Like him, you don't think that kissing between unmarried teenagers, openly gay youth leaders, or talking back to authority figures should be tolerated, much less rewarded with understanding and open discussion. Like him, making sure the children in your charge follow God's law is your highest priority. You especially admired the way he stood proudly for his religion, no matter what some other people in the room might have thought. After the town hall, you went home and Googled the Catholic academy the man was referring to. You loved what you saw—the orientation, if not the content. You started Googling around for parallel Muslim institutions and nearly jumped for joy when you found one. You have long been concerned that raising Muslim children in largely Christian environments will lead some of them to convert from Islam. Now you have a solution to both the presence of Christians and the negative aspects of American culture. All you have to do is convince some of the Muslim parents in the area to give it a try.

For a moment, let's switch back to the position of the Methodist minister.

You probably should not have hugged the imam, you think to yourself as you get into your car. The man was clearly uncomfortable with that. But come to think of it, he seemed uncomfortable the whole time. He barely moved when you respectfully extended your hand to shake his, he didn't look at you when you were talking, and he didn't respond to any of your ideas—ideas whose goal was to help people in your congregation better understand *his* religion.

Was it because you were an educated female religious leader? You turn the scene over in your mind, look at it from various angles, and conclude that the answer is inescapably yes. This frustrates you. Here you are reaching out to the newcomer community, just as you are called to do by the Gospel, and in return you get treated with sexist disrespect. You remember a male classmate at divinity school saying that women shouldn't be ministers. God had created men and women with different aptitudes and different roles. You and the other female divinity school students let him have it. Most of the men in the class supported you. You vowed to yourself that anytime sexism reared its ugly head, you would go after it. God created people equal; that is also the Gospel as you understand it. So, then, why hadn't you called out the Muslim imam when he was clearly giving off the vibe that you were a second-class citizen?

MICROENVIRONMENTS

Let's turn again and play a different role. Now I want you to imagine that you are the principal of the high school that the young Muslim and the young Methodist attend. The parents of the Muslim family came to see you a few months ago. You asked how they were adjusting to life in the town and they said quite well. As an African American who moved to this largely white community a decade back, you can sympathize with the position of the newcomer. The Muslim parents were very grateful for your support in letting their son out of class on Friday afternoons for prayer, and they are here to see you about another matter related to their faith. The food served in the cafeteria at school sometimes poses a problem. Once a week or so, the main item has pork in it—sausage pizza, pork hot dogs—and on those days, their kids came home hungry. Could the principal ensure that at least one main dish a day was pork-free? Abstaining from pork was an important part of their religion. Incidentally, the mother noted, most Jews do not eat pork either. So as this town and its school diversify, having a non-pork option will be good for both Jews and Muslims.

You thought this was a fine idea. You made the change and noted it in the weekly e-mail you sent to parents. That caused a problem that you did not foresee. A group of parents scheduled a meeting with you and accused you of caving to the demands of Sharia in the school. "Sharia?" you asked. "What does this have to do with Sharia?"

"Muslim law is evil," retorted one of the parents. "It starts with no pork and ends up with Christians getting executed."

This is sounding an awful lot like racism to you. These people have seen ugly things about Muslims on the evening news, and they are projecting that narrow information onto all the Muslims in the world. It's a dynamic that black people are all too familiar with.

"My sister married a Muslim," you tell the group of parents in your office. "He is a decorated officer in the United States Navy who respects my sister's Christian faith. She still goes to church every Sunday." That quiets them down for the moment, but you get the sense that this is not the last time you will have this conversation with this group.

You call your friend who is a high school principal in a far more diverse area, the kind of diversity that has yet to arrive in your town but is certainly coming. The two of you went to grad school together, and you had many discussions about the beauty of diversity and how excited you were to lead educational environments with teenagers and parents with a range of identities. You remember feeling a bit of envy when your friend got the job at the diverse high school. She would have a chance to put those grad school visions into practice.

Turns out that the reality is far more complicated than the dream. Your principal friend says that there are many wonderful things about the religious diversity of her school, but many frustrations as well. Increasingly, her school is balkanized by faith group—Jewish kids here, evangelical kids there, Muslims at their own table. During the most recent war in Gaza, a Jewish kid refused to be in the same math group as a Muslim, calling him a supporter of terrorism. The next morning, a bunch of lockers belonging to Jewish students were defaced, one with a Nazi symbol. During that time, some of the evangelicals wore shirts from the organization Christians United For Israel, forming close relationships with the Jews. But when a group of Reform Jewish girls came back wearing bracelets from a pro-choice rally, the evangelicals held a very public moment of silence for the victims of abortion, followed by a loud prayer asking "Jesus to forgive the sinners who support murder." That led to a screaming match in the girls' bathroom. During this same time, the Gay-Straight Alliance at the school was planning its annual event, and she had heard whispers that an evangelical-Muslim alliance was preparing a loud protest. To complicate matters further, a group of parents had started an "atheist parent support group," apparently frustrated that issues relating to religion were becoming an increasingly large part of the school culture. After a recent PTA meeting at which religious issues took up half the agenda, one of the atheist parents stood up and said that if this continued, he would sue the school for violating the separation of church and state. Before sitting down, he added, "Believing in religion is like believing in the Tooth Fairy. Grow up, people. Join the twenty-first century." It took ten full minutes to regain order after that zinger.

As you listen to your friend describe the situation in her high school, a couple of things occur to you. First, for all the talk about diversity in grad school, almost none of it had to do with the type of diversity you and your friend are now dealing with—religious diversity. This is not to say that the issues of race, class, gender, ethnicity, and sexuality are any easier to deal with, only that you expected those to be thorny and to be prepared for them. Listening to the stories your friend tells and knowing this diversity will come to your school sooner rather than later, you wish you had a framework for how to deal with conflicts based on diverse faith and philosophical convictions.

Second, while all the talk in grad school was about the beauty of diversity, your friend's stories illustrate that diversity isn't always or necessarily positive. As you read the paper the next morning, that point seems obvious to you. After all, many of the world's violent conflicts are between different religious groups within the same country or region. You find yourself repeating a simple line to yourself as if it's a revelation—diverse environments can quite easily become violent conflicts. You wonder why this was rarely framed as such in grad school.

You begin to do some reading on religious diversity as it relates to a microenvironment like a high school. You find the work of Diana Eck especially useful when it comes to a theoretical framework for religious diversity. Eck points out that phrases like "celebrate diversity" and "diversity is our strength" misunderstand the term "diversity," un-deservedly investing it with a positive meaning.[6] Diversity, according to Eck, ought to be understood as a neutral term with a range of possible consequences, everything from conflict to cooperation. When diversity is proactively engaged for positive ends, Eck calls it "pluralism." Simply put, diversity is a fact; pluralism is an achievement, one that must be worked at.

How do you positively engage diversity within a microenvironment like a high school to achieve pluralism? You and your principal friend used to assume that simply putting people with different identities in the same school with one another would somehow naturally facilitate positive relationships. In your own observations as a professional educator, that has never really held true. People self-segregate by identity group all the time. You see this at everything from seating at football games to seating in the lunchroom. Mostly this is harmless, but if a few kids from different identity groups have a beef with one another, too often their respective groups get involved and the conflict immediately escalates.

In your reading, you discover that there is scholarly literature on intergroup relations known as "contact theory." One of the key figures in this literature is Gordon Allport.[7] In his research, he discovered that simply throwing people with different identities into a microenvironment like a high school did not necessarily lead to good relationships between identity groups, especially those who had a history of tension or conflict. For positive relations to ensue, the microenvironment had to meet certain conditions: equal status between the parties, cooperation between the groups, common goals, and support by authorities.

In further reading into contact theory, you discover a study by Muzafer Sherif that illustrates Allport's theory.[8] Sherif and his team brought a group of boys to a summer camp called Robbers Cave. They separated the boys into two groups and organized activities intended to create intragroup solidarity and intergroup rivalry. The researchers intensified this polarization by giving preferential treatment to one group. They were surprised by how quickly the two groups of boys developed a sense of identity within their respective groups and antagonism to the other group. The hostility was so deep that violence broke out at some of the activities.

What really struck you as you read Sherif's work was how the researchers turned the situation around. The formula was simple, actually, and it pretty much followed Allport's theory: organize activities where the groups have to cooperate for a common goal. When the bus broke down on a trip to the swimming hole and the boys had to work together to get it out of a ditch, the sense of intergroup solidarity increased markedly.

You talk excitedly with your friends about your discoveries, and one of them refers you to the "Pal Al" section of Robert Putnam and David Campbell's book *American Grace*.[9] The book is a comprehensive look at American religion from the middle of the twentieth century to the present day. The question the authors seek to answer is how does a country that is both religiously diverse and devout, like the United States, avoid violent religious hostilities. The answer, they say, is that people in the United States have frequent occasions to develop positive, meaningful relationships with people from other religious communities. A friendship with even one member of a suspect or marginalized religious group can improve somebody's attitude toward the whole group. In fact, the Putnam and Campbell research showed that a friendship with someone from one minority religious group changes people's attitudes toward *other* minority religious groups. Befriending a Buddhist causes improved views toward Mormons, Muslims, and Hindus.

The lesson for your high school as its religious diversity increases is clear: be proactive about creating programs where students with diverse religious identities have to cooperate to achieve common goals. That is relatively easy to do at the student level. Everything from arts programs to volunteer projects to sports are possible level playing fields where cooperation is required, goals are shared, and lasting friendships can be formed. The problem is going to be with the parents and other community leaders. Will they (the all-important "authorities" that Allport says need to sanction the process) uniformly support these programs when some of them clearly have prejudices toward certain religious minorities?

MACROENVIRONMENTS

Finally, I want you to imagine yourself as the official leading the Department of Homeland Security's Faith Office. You have degrees in religion and international affairs, and your first posting was at the State Department, where your job was to advise the secretary of state on the various ways that religious issues were likely to have an impact on America's interests abroad. You switched over to the domestic side and came to lead the Faith Office at Homeland Security for two reasons: (1) you have a growing concern that conflict between religious groups abroad will cause tension between diaspora communities in the United States, and (2) the Department of Homeland Security oversees disaster relief efforts in the United States through the Federal Emergency Management Agency (FEMA). After the government and the Red Cross, faith-based groups like the Southern Baptists and the Salvation Army are the largest disaster relief organizations in the country.[10] In your time at the State Department, you saw diverse faith groups cooperate on a range of international disasters, momentarily putting their differences aside to provide aid to victims. If earthquakes could bring Christian, Muslim, and Hindu groups together in South Asia, then dealing with the aftermath of hurricanes might be a way of bringing diverse faith groups together in the American South. And if you do your job well, cooperating across religious lines after a disaster might be the first step to more long-term, sustained, interfaith relationships.

When you added religion to your international affairs major, your friends laughed at you. It was the 1990s and you were part of a group of ambitious, high-achieving students who harbored dreams of being senior diplomats. It was an especially heady time for you as a woman because Madeleine Albright was secretary of state. She was the first woman to hold the position, and you couldn't help but think to yourself: if she can do it, I can do it.

Most of your classes focused on how to build democratic institutions and transition from state-run economies to free markets in Eastern Europe. But you were taken by Samuel Huntington's 1993 *Foreign Affairs* article, "The Clash of Civilizations." Huntington believed that the increased interactions between people from different backgrounds brought about by globalization would heighten their sense of "civilizational identity." This dynamic would put deep differences into sharp relief. As Huntington wrote, "Differences among civilizations are not only real; they are basic. . . . The people of different civilizations have different views on the relations between God and man, the individual and the group, the citizen and the state, parents and children, husband and wife, as well as differing views of the relative importance of rights and responsibilities, liberty and authority, equality and hierarchy."[11]

Civilizational identities were made up of many things, but the most important element, according to Huntington, was religion. And religious differences, Huntington believed, ran especially deep and were particularly divisive. "Religion discriminates sharply and exclusively among people," he wrote.[12] Bottom line: the post–Cold War era, Huntington warned, would be dominated by religious conflict.

You agreed with Huntington's premise that religion mattered a great deal to a great many people and a smaller world brought those people into greater contact with one another, but you were skeptical about his conclusion that religious differences somehow had to lead to violent conflict. At least, you hoped that violence was not the inevitable consequence of increased interaction. Part of this was your reading of world affairs and part of it stemmed from being a devout Catholic. You rarely shared this part of your identity with your classmates and professors in the international affairs department. You had heard them scoff that religious people were part of "the flat earth society," and you had no desire to be thought ill of in that hypercompetitive environment. Still, you couldn't put away your religious identity when thinking about your policy positions. You remember how inspired you felt when you saw pictures of Pope John Paul II's trip to Poland in 1979, when he told the Polish people under Communist rule to "be not afraid." You were certain the pope's presence played a role in inspiring anti-Soviet movements in Poland. Maybe, as Stalin famously said, the pope did not command army divisions, but he certainly commanded people's hearts. And not just Catholic hearts. Growing up in a largely Methodist town, your best friend was another religious minority, a Muslim, and he was deeply moved by Pope John Paul II's visit to a mosque.

You were just beginning your career at the State Department when 9/11 happened. All of a sudden, Huntington was in vogue in foreign policy circles. People you knew were constantly quoting his line, "Islam has bloody borders." In your view, that was a dangerous conclusion to draw. No doubt the terrorism threat from certain Muslim groups was real, but Islam was an ancient, diverse tradition with 1.5 billion adherents. Looking at it entirely through the prism of terrorism was like looking at Catholicism only through the window of pedophile priests. You were happy that foreign affairs types were finally paying attention to religion, but you were concerned that the focus would be limited to a superficial and wrong-headed "Islam is dangerous" worldview.

A few months after 9/11, in February 2002, rioting in the western Indian state of Gujarat left a thousand Muslims dead. The more you read about the riots, the more you were convinced that they were not random bursts of emotion but a highly organized campaign by Hindu nationalist militias. There was even evidence of the government in Gujarat aiding and abetting horrific acts, like the rape of women and the burning of children. As an Indian American yourself, you had long taken pride in India's image as a religiously diverse nation whose disparate elements came together to form a larger whole. In fact, you saw profound similarities between India and the United States on this matter. But the combination of anti-Muslim violence in India and anti-Muslim prejudice in the United States was causing you concern for both the nation of your heritage and the nation of your citizenship.

You began to take a deep interest in how to ensure stability in religiously diverse democracies. One of the books that you found especially useful was *Ethnic Conflict and Civic Life*, Ashutosh Varshney's study of cities in India that experienced various kinds of tension between different religious groups. The key question Varshney asked was "Why do some cities explode in violence when tensions between different religious groups rise while other cities manage to remain peaceful?" The answer had everything to do with civic networks. Cities that had Rotary clubs, sports leagues, business groups, and other sorts of civic associations that brought together people from different faith groups managed to ride out religious tension without becoming violent (in Varshney's usage, the term "ethnicity" encompasses religious identity). Cities that did not have such networks were prone to deadly interfaith riots. As Varshney put it, "If engagement is only *intraethnic*, not interethnic, small tremors (unconfirmed rumors, victories and defeats in sports) can unleash torrents of violence. A multiethnic society with few interconnections across ethnic boundaries is very vulnerable to ethnic disorders and violence."[13] Networks of engagement don't fall from the sky; people build them. It was inspiring that India had civic leaders who took the time to create and nurture groups that brought people of different faiths together. If only there were more such leaders.

India was full of identity communities—ethnic, tribal, regional, linguistic—but it seemed as if religious identity had the most potent social impact. Why was that? It was reading the work of the sociologist Robert Putnam in preparation for taking the Homeland Security job that helped answer this question. In his landmark book *Bowling Alone*, Putnam points out that religious groups are likely the single largest source of social capital in American society. He writes, "Nearly half of all associational memberships in America are church related, half of all personal philanthropy is religious in character, and half of all volunteering occurs in a religious context."[14] Moreover, faith communities "provide an important incubator for civic skills, civic norms, community interests, and civic recruitment. Religiously active men and women learn to give speeches, run meetings, manage disagreements, and bear administrative responsibility."[15] While Putnam's study focused on the United States, your own experience traveling back to India indicated that faith groups there were enormous sources of social capital as well.

In his book *Better Together*, Putnam distinguishes between two forms of social capital in a diverse society. "Bonded" social capital is inward focused and frequently associated with a tight-knit identity group, like a religious community. "Bridged" social capital is outward facing and involves working together across lines of difference.[16] These two are not mutually exclusive. "Bonding" often generates the social capital used in "bridging." Think of a church group that gathers every Sunday for worship and every Wednesday for Bible study, and then one Saturday a month mobilizes its membership to participate in interfaith Habitat for Humanity building projects. The internal bonding of those Sundays and Wednesdays generates the social capital used for interfaith bridging on Habitat for Humanity Saturdays.

Both of these insights—the powerful social capital within religious groups, and the distinction between bonding and bridging social capital—shed light on the dynamics of India, and helped you prepare for your new role at Homeland Security in the United States. It was clear from Varshney's study that the deep pockets of social capital within religious communities in India cut two ways. On the one hand, in times of tension between those groups, this social capital (large groups of people who can be easily mobilized, physical spaces to hold events, money and other resources, an expectation of participation, leaders who are respected and heeded, social networking mechanisms that communicate quickly and broadly) turned quickly into the tools of interfaith violence. On the other hand, this exact same social capital can become the building blocks of a rich civic life for the broader city. A Muslim social networking site could be used to gather youth into a mosque for the purpose of rallying them to fight the Christians in the next neighborhood. That same communications technology and physical space can be used to organize a basketball tournament for young people from all backgrounds. The cities that were most prone to violence were the ones with the most bonded social capital and the least bridged social capital. When tensions ran high, bonded social capital—groups made up of people with a single strong identity—effectively served as easy-to-mobilize militias with guns pointed at the opposing identity group. Bridged social capital, on the other hand, interrupted, reduced, and prevented such violence.

A final study by Robert Putnam, titled "*E Pluribus Unum*," caught your eye. Putnam found that diversity, while not necessarily leading to violence, does have a negative impact on the broader community. He writes,

> Inhabitants of diverse communities tend to withdraw from collective life, distrust their neighbors, regardless of the color of their skin, to withdraw even from close friends, to expect the worst from their community and its leaders, to volunteer less, give less to charity and work on community projects less often, to register to vote less, to agitate for social reform more but have less faith that they can actually make a difference, and to huddle unhappily in front of the television . . . Diversity, at least in the short run, brings out the turtle in all of us.[17]

More than anything else, this study inspires you to be proactive in your leadership. Diversity, when left alone, tends toward isolation. This is bad for a participatory democracy, which relies on engaged citizens. Even more dangerous, the vacuum created by people withdrawing from public life is filled too easily by demagogues spreading the poison of prejudice and division. When divisive messages meet bonded social capital in an environment where diversity is unengaged, things can turn ugly fast, as the case of Gujarat in 2002 illustrates all too well. But there is another side to this social science. Proactive leadership can make a big difference. Finding ways to mobilize the networks within different religious communities for a common cause builds "networks of engagement" that bridge social capital and strengthen social cohesion. In disaster relief, you think you've found a cause that will inspire different religious groups to bring their particular networks to a common table, build bridges across lines of religious difference, make an impact on an issue they all care about, and strengthen America along the way. This last part you pull from Putnam's "*E Pluribus Unum*" study. While much of that paper is about the short-term negative consequences of diversity, toward the end Putnam highlights a key strategy for engaging diversity in a way that creates long-term benefits—shape a national narrative that includes people of all identities and encourages them to offer their particular contributions to the broader whole.

You get to work writing your invitation letters. You title the task force you are creating "Achieving America: An Interfaith Council for the Common Good." You begin each letter with a paragraph on how you have been personally inspired by that tradition's ethic of service. For the letters to Muslim leaders, you cite the Qur'an and the Hadith. For the letters to Jewish leaders, you cite the Torah and Rabbi Hillel. And so on. Your letter ends with a line from George Washington: "May the Lord of all mercies scatter light and not darkness and make each of us useful in our vocations and give us everlasting happiness in his own way." You want to remind people that at the heart of the American narrative is the belief that communities from the four corners of the earth, speaking different languages and praying in different ways (including never praying), can come together and build a nation. You wish Samuel Huntington had recognized that the best counterexample to the clash of civilizations was the possibility of America.

SUMMARY

We began this chapter with Peter Berger's key insight that modernity pluralizes, a dynamic that makes the inner lives of individuals highly complex because it shifts identity from fate to choice. Pluralization also puts pressure on religious communities, which no longer enjoy a taken-for-granted status and now must understand themselves as voluntary associations. Pluralization not only has implications for the identities of individuals and communities, but also makes relations between them a highly salient feature of the modern world. According to scholars like Samuel Huntington, increased interaction between people from different religious backgrounds is likely to lead to conflict, his famous "clash of civilizations." Other scholars like Robert Putnam find that

while diversity does not have to lead to conflict, it does tend to cause people to participate less in civil society. Such insights lead scholars like Diana Eck to draw a distinction between diversity and pluralism: diversity is simply the fact of people with different identities in intense interaction; pluralism is the achievement of understanding and cooperation.[18] For diversity to become pluralism, it must be positively and proactively engaged. It is especially important to engage religious diversity because of the social capital within religious communities and the bonding nature of religious identity. There are a variety of ways of engaging religious diversity positively. One is to create microenvironments where people from different backgrounds are more likely to cooperate together toward common goals and form prejudice-busting relationships in the process. Another is to proactively bridge the social capital (in Putnam's language) between religious groups by forming what Ashutosh Varshney calls "networks of engagement," or strong associations that involve people from different identity groups. Such networks not only strengthen social cohesion and bridge social capital, but have been shown to prevent violence. A final strategy for engaging diversity to build pluralism is to create an overarching narrative that includes a variety of groups and that encourages constituent communities to make contributions to the broader common good.

The character sketches that I provided illustrate the four most common ways of proactively responding to diversity: by building barriers or bunkers, by wielding bludgeons, or by carefully constructing bridges. Next, I briefly define each response and refer to how the characters I sketched in this chapter illustrate them.

Barriers

People who build barriers are interested in proudly proclaiming the righteousness of their identity and loudly denouncing other identities. They amplify differences and disagreements in a manner that is scornful of others. The attitude boils down to this: "In a world of different paths, I am on the one that is good and right. Everyone else is walking a road that is ugly and evil." The barrier response is best embodied by

the brother of the Methodist teenager who says he should not be friends with the Muslim, and by the Methodist youth who asks the pastor if the Bible says Islam is evil.

Bunkers

People who build bunkers want to seal themselves off from a world of diversity. Like those who build barriers, they believe their path is the best one, but they are neither overtly scornful toward others nor especially interested in accentuating differences. For the most part, they are not that interested in others at all. They are fully focused on preserving their own practices and traditions. The Muslim imam and the Catholic man who speaks at the town hall meeting are examples of people who seek to build bunkers.

Bludgeons

Those whose response to diversity is the bludgeon are violently antagonistic toward people who are different. Like those who build barriers, they are self-righteous about their own superiority, accentuating differences and scorning others. What distinguishes them from barrier builders is their willingness to use physical force to dominate those who are different. It's not "my way or the highway"; it's "my way or get beat over the head." Nobody in the sketches represents the bludgeon approach. Frankly, it is rare in contemporary American life. Muslim extremists like Al-Qaeda, the Islamic State, and the Taliban are the most common examples in our era of religious groups who respond to diversity with a bludgeon.

Bridges

There are several characters whose instincts are to respond to diversity by seeking to build bridges of understanding and cooperation. They experience various levels of frustration, opposition, and success. The Methodist teenager's mother thinks that being Christian means reaching out to the Muslim neighbor, but she has a hard time convincing her older son that her "bridge" interpretation of Methodist theology

is more correct than his "barrier" understanding. The Muslim parents showed their bridge-building instincts by emphasizing how Muslims share a service ethic with Christians and dietary restrictions with Jews, but they have yet to take concrete steps to actually build the bridge. The Methodist minister takes a risk and reaches out to the Muslim imam, but finds that some of her values (feminism, openness to change) are in tension with his views on those issues. The principal is reading social psychology research with an eye toward running programs that can create an environment in his high school that transforms diversity into pluralism. He can imagine how arts, sports, and volunteer projects will help his students but is stumped by the challenge from parents who will oppose this proactive approach, at least when it comes to Muslims. The final character, the Catholic woman who runs Homeland Security's Faith Office, also has a sound strategy. She is familiar with religious diversity frameworks through her reading of Huntington, Varshney, and Putnam. She is knowledgeable about both the service ethic in different religions and how this is put into practice in an area like disaster relief. Her "Achieving America" task force is a promising plan. She takes care to write letters that show respect for the particular service ethic in each faith tradition; highlights the relationship building that will take place while applying this service ethic in disaster relief efforts; and lifts up how their cooperation strengthens and celebrates the core American narrative of diverse groups working together. Will she have the skills to actually coordinate interfaith disaster relief efforts? After all, coming up with a plan is one thing; executing it is an entirely different thing. What happens if one of the faith groups that participates in the council begins to proselytize during one of the interfaith disaster relief efforts? What happens if a few of the groups send hundreds of volunteers and other groups send only a few? Does everyone get the same credit? These are the kinds of challenges inherent in real-world interfaith leadership.

A final note: In the metaphor at the center of this book, the "stones" of historical and theological knowledge are placed end to end to build interfaith bridges. But, in the vast realms of history and theology, one can easily find stones that are suited to form bunkers or barriers. And the same skills (public narrative, group facilitation) that connect stones into a bridge of cooperation can be used to turn those rocks into bludgeons of domination.

THREE

The "Faith" in Interfaith

When Wilfred Cantwell Smith accepted an appointment by the Canadian Overseas Missions Council to serve as a faculty member at Forman Christian College in Lahore in the early 1940s (then part of an undivided India under British rule, now a major city in Pakistan), he had little idea that the experience would change his understanding of Christian mission, Christian faith, and, as he titled one of his most widely read books, "patterns of faith around the world." These larger insights stemmed from a simple realization: most of the teachers and students at Forman were not Christian; they were Sikhs, Muslims, and Hindus. "The Christians among us," Smith observed, "were attempting to illustrate and live out our faith; our colleagues, participants in other traditions, often reverent individuals, were doing the same with theirs. They were happy to work with us, as we with them, towards constructing and maintaining a community—a friendly and cooperative community, religiously diverse."[1]

Had Smith been asked before he arrived what a Christian ought to do when put in the same room as someone of a different religion, he might well have answered, "Try to convert them." But when he found himself in a situation where he grew to respect people of other faiths as colleagues and, especially living in an unfamiliar country, rely on them as friends, he found other thoughts arising as well. How were they, together, to most effectively teach their students? What could they do, together, about the increasing religious violence in the subcontinent? What might he as a Christian learn from the faiths of the people around him?

In short, Wilfred Cantwell Smith was asking the types of questions that literally define the term "interfaith": What do my interactions with Sikhs, Muslims, and Hindus mean for my relationship with Christianity? And, how does my Christian faith influence the manner in which I interact with people who are Sikhs, Muslims, and Hindus?

Smith quickly realized that the diversity that characterized 1940s Lahore would not stay trapped there long. Modernity meant that the type of interfaith interaction he was experiencing at Forman Christian College would soon be the norm for cities worldwide. (Note the resonances with Peter Berger.) Smith viewed the growth of interaction between people who orient around religion differently as one of the great challenges of modern times: "The problem posed in this area is at least as important for humanity as that of nuclear physics; as intellectually challenging, as intricate, as exciting, as consequential."[2] And he realized that the field of religious studies was, at least in its mid-twentieth-century form, inadequate to the challenge.

The previous chapter took a deep dive into the "inter" half of interfaith. In this chapter, we look at the "faith" side. Smith's experience in Lahore is an ideal starting point because it highlights a situation in which the interaction between people of different identities clearly implicated their faith lives. It is important to emphasize that interfaith work is not simply about people with different religious identities in close quarters; that would characterize every grocery store, restaurant, and train station within five square miles of where I currently sit. Interfaith refers to situations where people with diverse faiths interact, *and their faith identities are somehow involved.*

Just as an exploration of interracial interaction requires a theory of the concept of "race," so a deep understanding of interfaith engagement requires a layered understanding of what "faith" means. Much of this chapter focuses on how Smith's definition of faith helps interfaith leaders do their work.

Before jumping in, I want to address the question: What is it about faith or religious identity that matters so much? The theologian Paul Tillich famously said that religion is about "ultimate concerns."[3] I understand ultimate concerns in two ways: the content of religious traditions, and the emotional force those traditions inspire in people. In other words, religious traditions contain elements that are ultimate in nature—stories of creation, views on human purpose, questions about salvation and the afterlife. And religious traditions energize people to invest a range of concerns that might normally be viewed as pedestrian with a sense of ultimacy. That is not just a group of people; that is the *ummah*, or the church, or the people of Israel. That is not just a piece of real estate; that is the place where Muhammad lifted off on his Night Journey, where the Second Temple once stood, where Jesus walked.

Different people are motivated in ultimate ways about different dimensions of religious traditions. Scripture motivates some in ultimate ways; for others, it is sacred place and peoplehood; and for others, it is rituals and ceremonies. Moreover, not only do people emphasize different dimensions of traditions, but they interpret and relate to those dimensions in very different ways. People in the Catholic Worker movement risk jail time to lead peace demonstrations with the hope of ending all wars. IRA militia members risk jail time to plant bombs for sectarian purposes. Though both claim to be Catholic, and both are motivated by elements of the tradition in ultimate ways, they emphasize different parts and interpret those parts in divergent ways.

Wilfred Cantwell Smith earned degrees from the University of Toronto, Cambridge, and Princeton. He found it frustrating that his studies in religion at all three universities cast little light on what he considered the most important issues raised by the religiously diverse environment of Forman Christian College. These included, in his own words, "learn[ing] to live together with our seriously different traditions, not only in peace but in some sort of mutual trust and mutual loyalty" and "arriving at a point . . . where we can appreciate others' values without losing allegiance to our own."[4]

The trouble with the academic study of religion, according to Smith, was that it focused too much on gathering data about the outward aspects of religions, under the assumption that this information would somehow automatically provide insight into the lives of that religion's followers. Smith finds this logic faulty, writing, "It is possible to know a great deal about what are called the various religious systems, and still not understand the people whose lives they help to form . . . It is one thing to know, for instance, that in Christian worship there is a cross; it is another to know what the cross means to the Christian who is worshipping."[5]

Smith's own primary concern was not with religious systems but with religious persons. After all, it wasn't Islam and Hinduism that had to get along at Forman; it was Muslims and Hindus. What type of inquiry might a religious studies scholar undertake to gain a deeper understanding of Muslims and Hindus? How might that inquiry be conducted to yield insights that would help them get along better?

To accomplish this, Smith makes four crucial moves. First, he separates what he calls the outward system of a religious tradition from the inner qualities that characterize individual adherents. The hajj is part of the outward system of Islam; one can show you the city of Mecca on a map and a picture of the Kaaba. But this approach does not give us much insight into the heart of any particular Muslim who is going through that experience.

This example sets up Smith's second move: addressing how to gain insight into the inner quality of an individual believer. Such a quality neither emerges entirely out of the individual's being nor magically drops from the doctrine or rituals of a religious system. Rather, the key is the relationship between the two, the manner in which the individual emphasizes and interacts with the various parts of the religious system—the Christian and the cross, the Muslim and the Kaaba, the Sikh and the Guru Granth Sahib. Smith sees this relationship between the adherent and the tradition as the central focus of his scholarly inquiry. He calls this relationship "faith."

The third move Smith makes is to suggest that one way to get a sense of the faith of a person is to observe how she expresses her relationship with her tradition in various daily contexts. To illustrate, Smith tells the story of a Muslim fruit seller he comes across while trekking in a remote area of the Himalayas. The man is using a handmade scale and some rocks to weigh the oranges he sells. Customers come by and order a pound or two of oranges; the fruit seller puts a certain number of rocks on his homemade scale, weighs them against the oranges, and states the price. None of his customers seem to have any problem with this. They watch the man put the oranges and the rocks on the scale, pay the stated price, and walk away with their fruit. Smith falls into conversation with the man and inquires about how this system is verified. The rocks have no markings that indicate their weight, and the scale is clearly not standardized. What prevents the man from overcharging his customers, Smith wonders. The fruit seller responds to Smith's question by quoting a verse from the Qur'an, "Lo, He over all things is watching." The implication is that this phrase requires of the fruit seller that he deal with his customers honestly. Moreover, his customers seem to know this about the fruit seller and, in the context of that small village, are willing to accept it as his bond.[6]

For Smith, the relationship between this man, the line in the Qur'an, and the manner in which he sold fruit is a perfect illustration of the concept of faith. The verse is part of the religious system called Islam, the man had a profound relationship with that particular verse, and the relationship expressed itself in the way he sold fruit. It is easy to imagine Muslims who cannot quote that particular verse from memory or might do so in a rote manner. They do not, for whatever reason, have a deep relationship with that particular line. Some might not quote the Qur'an at all but instead call attention to a particular Muslim saint and claim that the saint's example compels honesty. That Muslim is emphasizing a different dimension of the tradition of Islam. Some Muslims might intentionally overcharge their customers, thereby demonstrating a weak relationship with the parts of Islam that command honesty. This same person might punctiliously perform his five daily prayers. Some people who call themselves Muslims will emphasize some dimensions of the religious system called Islam, and other Muslims will emphasize other dimensions of the tradition.

This example also highlights Smith's fourth move—emphasizing social context. The fruit seller needed customers who were willing to accept that his honesty was guaranteed by a Qur'anic line. If the fruit seller was in a busy train station in the city of Bombay, rather than a small village in the Himalayas, his quoting of the sacred verse might not have been good enough for his customers. They might have demanded a standardized scale and proper weights rather than Qur'anic recitation. The social context of that Himalayan village allowed the Muslim fruit seller to express his faith in a particular manner.

There are, of course, myriad questions and critiques of Smith by his fellow comparative religions scholars. My purpose in presenting his understanding of faith is not to take sides in internal battles within a scholarly field. It is, instead, to underscore the key dimensions of an influential intellectual framework that is highly relevant for interfaith leaders. A friend of mine from grad school once told me: All models are wrong; some models are useful. For interfaith leaders, Smith's theory of comparative religions is extremely useful, especially in how it charts a middle course between two perennial arguments with regard to religious diversity.

ARE RELIGIONS MORE ALIKE OR MORE DIFFERENT?

The first argument can be summed up quite simply: are religions very different, or are they basically the same? Stephen Prothero is a key proponent of the "religions are very different" school of thought, and Karen Armstrong is an ardent defender of the "religions are essentially the same" view.

In the opening of his book *God Is Not One*, Prothero observes, "At least since the first petals of the counterculture bloomed across Europe and the United States in the 1960s, it has been fashionable to affirm that all religions are beautiful and true."[7] The most common metaphor for illustrating this view is the idea of Hinduism, Sikhism, Islam, Judaism, and so on being different paths up the same mountain, all leading to the same place. Prothero has little patience for this point of view, writing, "This is a lovely sentiment, but it is dangerous, disrespectful and untrue."[8] Religions diverge in many areas, including doctrine, ritual, and law. Christians don't go on pilgrimage to Mecca, Muslims do not find holiness in the cross, and Jewish law does not forbid alcohol, as Muslim law does. To dismiss these differences as the unimportant "foothills" in favor of the more magnificent summit is, for Prothero, "pretend pluralism."[9]

Perhaps the best known contemporary advocate for the view that religions are basically the same is the prolific author Karen Armstrong. Armstrong has sought to advance her view of religions being in essence the same through the Charter for Compassion project, which has captured the imagination of many people around the world. She says in her TED Prize talk that launched the Charter for Compassion, "It is an arresting fact that right across the board, in every single one of the major world faiths, the ability to feel with the other . . . is not only the test of any true religiosity, it is also what will bring us into the presence of what Jews, Christians and Muslims call 'God' or the 'Divine.' It is compassion, says the Buddha, which brings you to Nirvana."[10]

For Armstrong, this is most clearly illustrated in the fact that all the major religious systems have some version of what is generally known as the Golden Rule. The most commonly expressed version of this in the West is the Christian version: "Do unto others as you would have them do unto you." In that same speech, Armstrong highlights that Confucius articulated a version of the Golden Rule five centuries before Christ, telling his followers that the practice of "human-heartedness" would bring them to the transcendent experience of *ren*. Other articulations of the Golden Rule include: "None of you truly believes until he wants for his brother what he wants for himself," a saying of the Prophet Muhammad, and "That which is hateful to you, do not do to your neighbor," a teaching of Rabbi Hillel.

Wilfred Cantwell Smith's approach to the question of whether religions are very different or essentially alike is to highlight that all religions are made up of a myriad of dimensions, including doctrine, texts, rituals, ethics, community, art, and archetypal heroes. Different religious systems like Islam and Judaism are likely to be alike in some dimensions (the doctrine of monotheism and the primacy of sacred law) and different in other areas (whether God gave Jerusalem to Muslims or Jews). But, as it is people who relate, interpret, and give expression to various dimensions of religious systems, the real question is, "Are Muslims and Jews forming relationships with the dimensions of their traditions that are more alike, or the dimensions that are more different?" And as context matters greatly, the question for interfaith leaders is: "Given that there are dimensions of Islam and Judaism that are similar and those that are different, what can I do to encourage Muslims and Jews to highlight the dimensions that are similar? What stories might I emphasize? What spaces might I create? What activities might I organize?"

Let me illustrate with a personal story. When I was eight or nine years old, I received an invitation to the birthday party of one of the more popular boys in class. I was over the moon. On the morning of the party, my mother noticed that the invitation said that Danny's parents would be making hot dogs for lunch. As my mother was not sure whether the hot dogs were beef or pork, and as not eating pork was an important part of our Muslim identity, my mother sent me to Danny's party with two beef hot dogs in a plastic bag and instructions to politely ask his parents to heat them up in a separate (unporked) pan. I was nonplussed. I did not relish being the brown boy with the beef hot dogs at the popular kid's birthday party. But obeying my parents was also a part of my being Muslim (and being eight), so I looked for ways to hide the hot dogs on my body (an inelegant and nearly impossible task) and went off to the party.

When lunchtime came, I found a way to sneak away from the crowd and into the kitchen, where I slunk into a corner with my little plastic baggie. I discovered, to my surprise, that somebody had beat me to the spot. In that corner stood another little boy doing his best to hide a plastic bag that carried two hot dogs.

"Who are you?" I asked.

"My name is Chaim," he replied. "My mom made me bring beef hot dogs," he said, reluctantly holding up the plastic bag.

"Are you Muslim?" I asked, somewhat incredulous.

"No," he said. "I'm Jewish."

I remember having two dominant thoughts at that time: This kid and me, we were going to be friends. And whatever "Jewish" was, I liked it.

It is interesting to note that many of my closest friends have been Jewish. Of course, that single incident didn't cement those friendships, but it did positively incline me from an early age. From that point on, when I met a Jew, I assumed we had similarities, and I assumed those similarities had something to do with how we related to our respective religions.

For me, the lesson of this story is simple: a particular environment made salient a commonality in faith between Chaim and me. A different environment may have elicited different expressions of our faith, expressions that could have highlighted divisions rather than resonances. What if, for example, our parents had taken us to dueling demonstrations on the Middle East, me joining most other Muslims on the pro-Palestinian side and Chaim joining most other Jews on the pro-Israeli side? That environment would have made other dimensions of our traditions salient, and that first meeting could very well have been marked by bitter antagonism rather than friendship.

An important part of what interfaith leaders do is construct environments that highlight similarities in faiths across diverse people and groups, therefore making cooperation more likely.

RELIGIOUS OR SPIRITUAL?

Wilfred Cantwell Smith's theories also help us chart a middle path between two poles on the question of what kind of participants interfaith leaders should recruit, those who represent religious traditions or those who define themselves as individualistically spiritual?

People at the first pole are exponents of a framework that, for my purposes here, I will associate with Will Herberg's famous 1955 book *Protestant-Catholic-Jew*.[11] Herberg called mid-twentieth-century America a "triple melting pot" with religious identity as the primary social marker. Herberg regarded the three communities he writes about as equally American (a significant social improvement from the Protestant domination of previous eras), and viewed them as enclosed and monolithic. He was generally blind to differences within traditions, making little mention of ethnic diversity in the Catholic Church, racial differences among Protestants, or the various theological movements in Judaism. And he portrayed an America where the three communities essentially lived parallel lives in their separate religious circles, meeting one another only by intentional effort.

Herbergians recognize that many more religions are now represented in the United States, but effectively take religious diversity to mean "Catholics, Protestants, Jews, Hindus, Muslims, Buddhists, and the like." They tend to project Herberg's mid-twentieth-century model of communities as enclosed and monolithic onto the early-twenty-first-century American landscape.

The spiritual perspective is perhaps best embodied by the famous example of Sheilaism from the classic book coauthored by Robert Bellah, *Habits of the Heart*. In describing her understanding of cosmic matters, Sheila tells the research team, "I believe in God . . . I am not a religious fanatic. I can't remember the last time I went to church. My faith has carried me a long way. It's Sheilaism. Just my own little voice . . . It's just love yourself and be gentle with yourself. You know, I guess, take care of each other."[12]

Bellah and his coauthors note that Sheila likely once belonged to a community or tradition, or at least is familiar with one, but does not engage with it now. She is unwilling to state anything more specific about her faith or spiritual worldview than what I've quoted.

The religious/Herbergian approach to interfaith cooperation pictures a person from the Protestant house visiting a person in the Jewish house for tea. This is not really how we live today. There are many stripes of Protestants and Jews (and Mormons and atheists and Daoists), and rarely do they live in highly separate enclaves. As I wrote in chapter 2, we interact with much more frequency than Herberg's model suggests, which means the model of leaving one religious enclave to visit another is not an accurate image of interfaith cooperation.

The Herbergian approach privileges people in the formal hierarchy of religious systems, typically scholars or clergy, viewing them as more authentic and powerful representatives of communities and traditions. This discriminates against the vast majority of people who are not part of a formal religious hierarchy, and it discourages those who do not (for very good reasons) desire to represent entire systems. Furthermore, it demands of traditions that do not have formal religious hierarchies in the manner of, say, the Catholic Church that they pretend to.

The language used by this interfaith approach betrays its biases. Take the oft-quoted statement by the renowned Catholic theologian Hans Küng, which has become a kind of Lord's Prayer of a certain kind of interfaith cooperation: "No peace between the nations without peace between the religions. No peace between the religions without dialogue between the religions."[13] As "religions" don't do things, they must be represented by creatures who do, namely, people. And the kind of people that Küng undoubtedly has in mind are people quite like him, with titles before their names (Rabbi, Reverend, Father) and plenty of letters after (SJ, PhD, JD).

The spiritual/Sheila approach is more common among younger people and at the grassroots level, in the form of book groups and college campus "meaning making" conversations. This approach often takes pride in involving people at some distance from "world religion" systems, including those who have an oppositional attitude toward religious tradition. While more open to a range of people and diverse spiritual expressions than the more formal approach I've described, it can turn off people who are a part of such traditions or have respect for the hierarchies within them.

Smith's middle path emphasizes, with Herberg, that religious traditions and their corresponding communities do in fact exist and matter a great deal. It parts ways with Herberg by emphasizing the internal diversity of these traditions, rather than viewing them as monoliths. Moreover, Smith would vehemently disagree with the Herbergian understanding of individuals as formal ambassadors of religious systems. In this sense, Smith would likely agree with Sheila's insistence that she herself is the agent of meaning making, but he would disagree with her notion that she generates this meaning out of thin air. Instead, he would encourage Sheila to see the symbols and forms that she makes meaning with—a favorite hymn, perhaps, or a cherished object like prayer beads—as dimensions of a larger tradition.

Part of the reason that these two approaches continue to organize interfaith work is that there is some coherence to each. In the religious/ Herbergian approach, your ticket in is a recognizable religious label. There are some benefits to this. The various labels—Muslim, Hindu, Mormon, Jain—can all be organized under the familiar category "religion," and programs can be structured from this straightforward organizing category. The drawback is that it pretends that the only patterns of difference that matter are the "world religion" categories.

The spiritual/Sheila approach has the advantage of being, on the surface, open to a wider range of people. In reality, however, it tends to discourage people who do claim clear labels and strong religious commitments. Furthermore, unlike the religious/Herbergian approach, it is hard to think of a good way to organize an interfaith program in the spiritual/Sheila approach. My experience of such gatherings involved plenty of unsatisfying and meandering discussions and, I kid you not, quite a bit of interpretive dance. Without organizing categories like "religion," the facilitators couldn't think of much else for the group to do together. In my mind, the biggest problem with the spiritual/Sheila approach is that it pretends that there are no religious or spiritual patterns at all.

WHAT WE TALK ABOUT WHEN WE TALK ABOUT RELIGIOUS DIVERSITY

Herberg was undoubtedly onto something when he broke apart the myth of a Protestant America and spoke of the multiple world religion communities that had social significance within the country. But to pretend that world religion is the only pattern of identity and interaction that matters is to live in a time warp, and a two-dimensional one at that. Yet to fully embrace the Sheila paradigm and chase around hundreds of millions of patterns won't work either.

The question boils down to this: when it comes to religious diversity, what patterns of identity and interaction should interfaith leaders pay attention to? I want to suggest four:

1. The first pattern to pay attention to is the *world religions category*. I've written much about this already, so I won't elaborate more here. Suffice it to say that the labels Sikh, Buddhist, Hindu, and so on matter a great deal to a great many people.

2. The second pattern is *intrafaith diversity*, the doctrinal variety within every tradition and community. Within Christianity, there are Catholics and Protestants. Within Protestants, there are "mainline" and "evangelical." Within "mainline," there are Episcopalians, Presbyterians, Methodists, ELCA Lutherans, and members of the United Church of Christ. These various distinctions emerged because enough people emphasized different elements of doctrine within the broader tradition and generated the energy to build communities around those distinctive elements. Shia Muslims emphasize the Prophet Muhammad's appointment of Ali as the first imam and next leader of the Muslim community. Sunni Muslims do not. This doctrinal difference resulted in the emergence of different communities within the tradition of Islam. There is a similar story in just about every religion. Because these doctrinal communities constitute a major pattern of identity, interfaith leaders have to pay attention to them, and not just the broader world religion system from which they emerge.

3. The third pattern is *intersectional identities*. Nobody is defined entirely by his or her religious identity. Even if religion may be highly salient, it is always intersecting with other identities like race, class, gender, geography, politics, ethnicity, nationality, and sexuality. Interfaith leaders have to recognize how intersecting identities influence patterns of being, believing, and belonging. Consider all the various identities that made up Ruth Messinger in 1964—white, female, Jewish, graduate school educated, social worker, politically liberal, and raised in a financially

comfortable environment in New York City. Think also of the
various identities of Ruth's partners. Certainly their evangelical Christian faith was a primary identity, but their location in
western Oklahoma no doubt had something to do with their
response to Ruth's overtures, and the fact that they lived in
houses gave them the class privilege to offer up those houses as
foster homes. Not all identities matter equally for the purpose
of interfaith intersectionality. Being a middle child might be an
important identity for many, and there is certainly a rich psychological literature on it, but there is no "middle child church"
or "middle child theology" the way there is a "black church"
and "feminist theology." Two vectors of intersectionality seem
especially important to highlight.

- The first is political. Robert Putnam and David Campbell
  write in *American Grace* about how meaningful religious
  divisions in the United States are not so much between
  Christians and Jews but between people who, at one pole,
  are politically conservative and highly devout across religions and those, at the other pole, who are politically liberal
  and lightly devout or secular. Putnam and Campbell even
  find evidence that political ideology drives religious choice,
  meaning that someone who is politically conservative is more
  likely to leave a liberal church for a conservative one rather
  than change her politics.[14] This matters for interfaith leaders
  because it means that the most significant fault line to emerge
  in an interfaith discussion group may be between a Protestant who goes to church three times a week and is pro-life,
  and a Protestant who goes to church three times a year and
  is pro-choice.

- The second type of intersectional diversity I want to underscore is embracing multiple religious traditions, or *Being
  Both*, as Susan Katz Miller calls it in her recent book. Miller
  points out the significant swath of Americans who are in
  interfaith marriages or live-in relationships, 37 percent

according to a 2008 Pew survey, a number that has surely risen since then. Many members of this group are part of what Miller calls "a grassroots movement of interfaith families claiming the right to create their own communities beyond a single creed or dogma, bound instead by respect for both Judaism and Christianity and a desire to explore the theological similarities, differences and points of historical and theological connection."[15] This is a growing category that interfaith leaders need to recognize and pay attention to.

4. The fourth distinct pattern I want to highlight are the *religious nones*. Twenty percent of Americans check "none" on religious identity surveys, and among millennials, the number is 33 percent and seems to be rising. There are three groups within this category that I want to highlight. The first and most obvious are the ardent atheists, largely because of the best-selling books and loud voices associated with this identity published over the past several years. But numerically atheists are relatively small. A larger group within the nones comprises people who might be called seekers or spiritual but not religious, people who resemble Bellah's Sheila. The nones also contain the growing number of people who proactively seek community with others who share their secular values. These communities often mirror many important dimensions of religious traditions, while maintaining intentionally nonreligious ethics. Secular humanism has central texts and prominent heroes and is increasingly creating formal communities and rituals for important life events like birth, marriage, and death.[16] Language is a challenge when it comes to this category, in part because it contains a wide diversity of people and in part because sociologists have only recently paid attention to those who were unwilling to place themselves into world religion categories in surveys. It seems pretty straightforward that few people wish to be known as a none. But beyond that agreement, there are only arguments. Ronald Dworkin, in *Religion Without God*, maintains that employing

the word "religious" for those who marvel at the mystery of the universe but do not believe in God is useful; "expanding the territory of religion improves clarity by making plain the importance of what is shared across that territory."[17] For myself, for now, I will stick with Wilfred Cantwell Smith, the guiding light of this chapter, who addresses nontheistic worldviews and maintains that the word "faith" is still relevant: "Simply to be a theist is by no means to be a person of faith. To be a non-theist is by no means not to have faith . . . faith is sensitivity and response, to the intangibles of ultimate worth."[18] We approach such intangibles through the tangible dimensions of traditions, whether the birth rituals of Judaism or the communal picnic of a secular humanist society.

THE VALUE OF TRADITIONS

To conclude, I want to address the question Why should interfaith leaders emphasize tradition at all, religious or otherwise? Given that interfaith leadership is about the people not the systems, why not treat all comers as individuals, as Sheilas? If they want to connect themselves to a tradition, fine. If not, that's fine, too. Why be forward about the system?

This is a complicated question. Part of the answer is that many, many people do in fact locate their identity and energy in connection to a system or tradition. Being forward about the question is simply giving them permission to talk openly about something that matters greatly to them. A second reason is that many of the things through which spirituals/Sheilas make meaning are, in fact, part of traditions, but are not recognized as such. For example, I've met many people who tell me that although they were raised Catholic, they have no connection to the tradition whatsoever. And then they say that they find themselves enormously inspired by Pope Francis. It seems to me that there is value in gently suggesting that Pope Francis is actually very much a part of the Catholic tradition. The office he holds, the name he chose, the manner in which he speaks, the reasons underlying his views—all these things are actually quite Catholic. If you find Pope Francis life giving, perhaps you will find some other dimensions of the Catholic tradition life giving as well. It doesn't hurt to issue the invitation.

The reason for this is because religious traditions generate significant social value. Mary Jo Bane, Brent Coffin, and Richard Higgins offer six ways in the introduction to their book, *Taking Faith Seriously* (they use the terms "faith" and "religion" interchangeably, which would have given Wilfred Cantwell Smith heartburn): [19]

- Fostering expression
- Forming identities
- Creating social bonds
- Shaping moral discourse
- Enabling participation
- Providing social services

I happen to be writing in the wake of a national tragedy, leavened by stunning acts of faith-inspired goodness, goodness that illustrates in perfect poetry the somewhat stiff typology of the six ways listed.

On June 17, 2015, a small group of parishioners at Emanuel AME Church in Charleston, South Carolina, gathered for the regular Wednesday night Bible study.[20] About a dozen of them sat around a green table, sang hymns, offered prayers, and reflected upon verses 4:16–20 from the Gospel of Mark.

The regulars at Mother Emanuel Church were joined that night by a visitor, a twenty-one-year-old white man with a mop of stringy hair. Dylann Roof had knocked on the door of the church, asked for the pastor, and been welcomed to the Bible study. It was somewhat unusual to have a young white man drop in for a Wednesday night Bible study at a black church, but the congregants believed that God's grace is open to everyone all the time. The senior pastor, the Reverend Clementa Pinckney, sat the young man in an honored place, right next to him.

It was not until the end of the Bible study, when Dylann Roof took out his .45-caliber Glock semiautomatic pistol and started shooting that his intentions were made plain. "You don't have to do this," Tywanza Sanders, a twenty-six-year-old barber, pleaded with the gunman.[21]

"You rape our women. And you're taking over our country," Dylann Roof responded. "I have to do this."[22] At the end of the terror, nine people were dead, including Mr. Sanders and the Reverend Pinckney.

In the hours after, America seemed to sway between barely contained anger and shocked silence. It was the community that had been most affected who somehow managed grace.

Thirty-six hours after the shooting, at a bond hearing that took place over closed-circuit television, family members of the dead confronted the murderer of their loved ones. "I forgive you," Nadine Collier said to her mother's killer, who wore striped prison garb and a blank expression. "I will never talk to her ever again, never be able to hold her again. I forgive you, and have mercy on your soul. You hurt me, you hurt a lot of people, but I forgive you."[23]

Alana Simmons, whose grandfather Daniel Simmons was killed by Dylann Roof, said, "Everyone's plea for your soul is proof that they lived in love and their legacies live in love."[24]

The Sunday after the shooting, Mother Emanuel Church held services without its senior pastor. Those who knew him, like the Reverend Jermaine Watkins of Journey Church, climbed into the pulpit and spoke words like this:

> To hatred, we say no way, not today. To racism, we say no way, not today. To reconciliation, we say yes. To a racial war, we say no way, not today. To racial fear, we say no way, not today.[25]

How is it that family and community members could, so soon after the most heinous attack imaginable, forgive the perpetrator and focus on reconciliation? The answer, according to the Aspen Institute's Eric Motley, is obvious: religious tradition. In a beautiful piece for the Aspen Institute's website, Motley explains how the relationship of the congregants of Mother Emanuel to the various dimensions of the Christian tradition gave them equanimity in the wake of their unspeakable tragedy.[26] His essay illustrates every one of the six points in Bane, Coffin, and Higgins's list.

Motley writes of the "timeless values" instilled by Wednesday night Bible study, sessions that he attended regularly growing up. He credits those Bible sessions with giving him his identity. "We discussed what was happening around us and in our lives," he recalls, "and we looked at those events with a collective wisdom shaped by our biblical understanding of history and human nature . . . The themes of love, faith, hope, and forgiveness were the biblical cornerstones of our collective journey, reminding us that love is the law of life."

Note the emphasis on the word "collective," and the highlighting of Christian moral discourse. For Motley, this foundation of strong community combined with cosmic narrative in the tradition of Christianity inspired family members of the Charleston nine with the strength to show up—to participate—and provided them a moral lexicon from which to choose their words.

Motley quotes from the theologian Reinhold Niebuhr: "We must be saved by the final form of love, which is forgiveness." He interprets this to mean that "our forgiveness of others is supposed to be an expression of God's divine forgiveness to us." It was this standard that the congregants of Mother Emanuel were living out.

It does not escape Motley that "secular culture," in the wake of the tragedy-forgiveness epic in Charleston, had lauded Mother Emanuel's long history of social action: serving as a stop on the Underground Railroad, nurturing a slave revolt, hosting Martin Luther King Jr., giving out food baskets to poor people in the community. This same secular culture, Motley notes, often looked at the regularity of Sunday morning church services and Wednesday night Bible study "sneeringly and dismissively." But it is precisely these rituals that undergirded the more above-the-surface, celebrated, and quantifiable social contributions of religious communities.

The power of a religious tradition, Motley points out, is the connections it cultivates between things like identity formation, the building of social bonds, and the nurturing of moral discourse. Engaging in the tradition trains the ethic of grace into your spiritual muscle memory, giving you strength to participate when you'd rather stay home, the words to say when you are speechless. "In this moment of grief, and in the rest of our trouble-filled lives, it is our faith that sustains us, with the hope of transcendence," Motley writes.

That is why attention to traditions, in relationship to the people that they sustain, matters.

VISION

Where should the bridge of interfaith cooperation lead? There are re-markably divergent answers to this question among people involved in interfaith work. Part of the challenge of an interfaith leader is to artic-ulate a clear vision for where she is taking a group of people who are risking a journey across a bridge on a highly complex interfaith land-scape. The following chapter presents a way of understanding the des-tination, a description of how the landscape changes as you approach it, and a handy tool for helping you make sure you are heading in the right direction.

FOUR

The Vision of Interfaith Leadership

Interfaith cooperation means many things to many people. Here are some of the more pointed views I have come across in recent years:

- *At a meeting of highly respected religious leaders, I rattle off the diverse identity groups involved in Interfaith Youth Core programs. When I get to humanists, one leader stops me and says, "Wait, did you just say that you've got people who don't believe in God involved in your organization? Isn't the purpose of interfaith work to unite believers against nonbelievers, especially now, in an era of advancing secularism?"*
- *In the question-and-answer session following my speech at a small college in the Midwest, a young woman stands up and asks, "How long do you think it will take interfaith work to achieve its goal of ushering in a postreligious society?"*
- *At a dinner with progressive Christians in New York City, someone comments that the political alliance between Jews and evangelical Christians regarding Israel is fascinating. The face of one of the dinner guests grows dark and stormy. She*

exclaims angrily, "An alliance dedicated to injustice can never be truly interfaith."

- *At the benefit event for a significant Jewish institution in Chicago, I am introduced to someone as a person who builds interfaith cooperation on college campuses. She says, "Oh, so you are doing something to stop the bigots running anti-Israel campaigns!"*

- *After a talk at a progressive church in Portland, a woman stands up, joins her palms in a form of prayer, and asks, "At what point in your interfaith journey did you learn that all religions were true and one? When do you share this wisdom with others?"*

- *In a conversation with a Muslim at a conference on Islam, he says, "When during your interfaith work do you invite people into the one right religion—Islam?"*

- *During a session with campus leaders at a public university in Utah, where the population is 85 percent Mormon, someone suggests an idea for an interfaith program: returned Mormon missionaries should give presentations about their missions to religiously diverse audiences in addition to Mormon groups. This way the Truth will be heard by many kinds of people.*

- *Right after this person speaks, a woman stands up and says she loves interfaith work because it recognizes that there is no such thing as a single capital "T" Truth, but instead many small "t" truths.*

As you can see, not only are these definitions different, they are in conflict with one another. People on both sides of various divides see the term "interfaith" as a vehicle for their view. When pro-Israel folks hear the term "interfaith," they think, "Support for Israel." When critics of Israel hear "interfaith," they think, "Criticism of Israel." Committed theists who are concerned with the rise of the numbers of nonreligious want interfaith to be about uniting believers to defeat nonbelievers. Nonbelievers who are concerned with the influence of religious voices often want interfaith to be about eradicating religious belief.

The first thing to say about this is that it is par for the course. When people with diverse religious identities gather under a banner as [neb-ulously] defined in the public imagination as "interfaith" is, it should come as no surprise that they bring their own meanings to the term, and that those meanings represent their particular identities, views, and biases.

An interfaith leader ought to look at this situation the way a mountain climber looks at a mountain. The first reaction is not, "Hey, how did *that* get there?" It is, "I *came* to climb this mountain."

Similarly, when an interfaith leader realizes that there is confusion and conflict in the room, including about the meaning of the term "interfaith," the adrenaline should start pumping and the excitement should grow. You prepared for this; it is a natural part of the landscape. What do you think interfaith work is but a gathering of people with diverging views on matters of ultimate concern? And if the first issue up for discussion is the meaning of the term "interfaith," is it any surprise that the diverse views and identities people carry get projected onto that?

The problem interfaith cooperation seeks to solve is precisely the one highlighted by the conflicting definitions people bring to the term—how to get people with opposing religious views in a democracy to engage positively. In the metaphor of bridges and landscapes, this chapter describes the place on the landscape of religious diversity where the bridge of interfaith cooperation leads, a place called pluralism.

PLURALISM

As discussed earlier, Harvard scholar Diana Eck makes a hugely useful distinction between the term "diversity" and the term "pluralism." Diversity, she claims, is simply the fact of people with different identities interacting with one another. In and of itself, diversity is neither good nor bad; it is simply a demographic fact.[1] Diversity can be very positive; imagine the variety of people who came together to fight for civil rights in mid-twentieth-century America. It can also turn into something highly destructive. Consider the conflicts between different religious identities over the past half century in the Balkans, South Asia,

Northern Ireland, the Middle East, and Central Africa. When diversity turns in a negative direction, it is generally characterized by prejudice, discrimination, and conflict, the barriers and bludgeons I wrote about in chapter 2.

Pluralism, on the other hand, is the energetic engagement of diversity toward a positive end. Where diversity is a fact, pluralism is an achievement.

In the same vein, the Jesuit theologian and political philosopher John Courtney Murray further defines pluralism thus:

> [The strength of pluralism is in] the coexistence within the one political community of groups who hold divergent and incompatible views with regard to religious questions—those ultimate questions that concern the nature and destiny of man within a universe that stands under the reign of God. Pluralism therefore implies disagreement and dissension within the community. But it also implies a community within which there must be agreement and consensus. There is no small political problem here. If society is to be at all a rational process, some set of principles must motivate the general participation of all religious groups, despite their dissensions, in the oneness of the community. On the other hand, these common principles must not hinder the maintenance by each group of its own different identity.[2]

The examples that opened this chapter provide a useful illustration for key concepts in the theories of Eck and Murray. The various definitions of the term "interfaith" highlight the *diversity* gathered, including the *divergent* and *incompatible* views people within the group held. For this diversity to achieve *pluralism*, an interfaith leader has to *engage* the group in a manner that accommodates the deeply held identity differences and the inevitable conflicts these differences imply, while at the same time building *agreement, consensus, and general participation* in the oneness of the community.

These concepts have helped me develop a three-part framework for pluralism: respect for identity, relationships between different communities, and a commitment to the common good.

✳ Respect for Identity ✳

Respect for identity has three main parts. The first is that people have a right to form their own identities regarding religion, or anything else for that matter. They can be believers or nonbelievers, Christians or Muslims, Sufis or Salafis. Moreover, they can be pro–gay marriage, black feminist Christians or anti–gay marriage, black feminist Christians.

Second, people have a right to express their identity. They can pass out flyers about their views at the bus stop. They can form civic associations that nurture their patterns of believing, behaving, and belonging. And they can seek to influence politics—voting for particular candidates, raising money for favorite causes, running for office on their chosen platform—in the direction of their identity-based views.

Third, people's identities should be reasonably accommodated. This means everything from adequate facilities for the observance of various religious practices, to a basic education about the diversity of identities within a society.

To respect someone else's identity does not require you to agree with it or to accept it. A Muslim who believes that Muhammad is God's final prophet can respect a Bahá'í without accepting Bahá'u'lláh as a prophet. That Muslim, if she is the facilities manager at the company where that Bahá'í works, needs to provide reasonable accommodation for his prayers and recognize that he might wish to express his faith by offering a lunch-and-learn discussion in the company cafeteria. In my view, she ought to attend this presentation to learn more about the Bahá'í tradition. She can disagree with a part of Bahá'í doctrine and still learn to appreciate other dimensions of the tradition, for example, the beautiful architecture of Bahá'í temples.

Relationships Between Different Communities

In a diverse society, if people have the right to both form and express identities, those various identity expressions will undoubtedly find themselves in conflict, as indeed they do in our own diverse society. Respect is fundamental in this situation, but I do not think it is sufficient. It is easy to imagine a situation where the Muslim facilities manager grudgingly allows the Bahá'í to place his scriptures on his desk and in the common library of the company (certainly if other scriptures like the Bible and Qur'an are available there), yet maintains a chilly distance in all other relations. Multiply that scenario across identity groups and you have the definition of tribalism and a recipe for conflict.

If the chief virtue in our diverse society is respect for identity, we are in danger of becoming a nation where people accommodate those with whom they disagree but have little else to do with them. They keep their most substantive conversations only within circles of the like-minded. When there is a serious disagreement on a principle with public implications—abortion, same-sex marriage, Middle East politics—on which one group decides it cannot respect a divergent view, the absence of relationships means the potential for conflict is high.

Even if violent conflict does not actually erupt, grudging respect and chilly distance between identity communities is not a particularly inspiring vision for a diverse society. It views diversity as a problem to be mitigated rather than a good to be approached with warm, if considered, embrace. That is one reason that building relationships between diverse communities is a second key principle of pluralism. By "relationship," I mean positive, constructive, warm, caring, cooperative engagement. This takes the form of conversation, activity, civic association, and friendly contact. It almost always involves some dimension of concern for the other's well-being. These are not connections based on the fiction of total agreement across all dimensions of identity, but rather engagement in full awareness that there are areas of both commonality and divergence and a commitment to care for one another in recognition of both.

Let me illustrate with a simple, relatable example. My wife's parents are moderately observant Muslims. For many years, they lived in a Chicago suburb next to an evangelical Christian family who homeschooled their three girls. At first, the two families were pleasant to each other but had little contact. Things changed when, after Eid prayers one year, our two sons were running around in their grandparents' backyard and the girls next door poked their heads over the wooden fence and invited them to play. Our boys whooped happily and went. This, of course, meant all of us adults—my wife and me, and my wife's parents—trooped across the driveway, knocked on the door, and properly introduced ourselves to the neighbors. We collectively overheard a fascinating interfaith conversation in the backyard, our oldest son, Zayd, explaining that he got out of school today to celebrate Eid, a holiday that Muslims believe in because we believe in the Prophet Muhammad and the Qur'an. The neighbor's oldest daughter responded that they go to school at home so they can follow a Christian curriculum because they believe in Jesus and the Bible. We adults shifted uncomfortably, knowing full well the doctrinal issues at stake. "Looks like someone learned something in religion class this week," somebody commented, allowing nervous laughter to break out.

The interfaith conversation in the backyard continued, the kids sharing back and forth about their religions, including the differences and contradictions. None of the adults stepped in to stop it; the things that were being said were true, and important. I think we probably all felt a little flush of pride that our kids were proud enough of their religions to speak about them openly to strangers. The adults chose to relate on different things.

"How often do your kids come here?" the woman next door asked my wife.

"About once a month or so," my wife said.

"Please send them over to play. My girls really want playmates and your boys are so sweet. Hey, I just made muffins. Can I offer you some?" she asked.

We, of course, said yes. My mother-in-law responded that there was going to be plenty of food left over from our Eid feast; she would bring some by later.

Over the next several years, lots of baseball was played between the kids, many baked goods were exchanged, recommendations for the best local plumbers were shared, and a handful of interfaith conversations (mostly between the kids) were had. When Chicago experienced record-breaking cold, my father-in-law felt more comfortable leaving for an out-of-town business trip, knowing that his wife would be looked after in case of frozen pipes or a dead car battery, because of the relationship with their neighbors. When the woman next door had to run out to get something from the grocery store, my mother-in-law would watch her kids for a few minutes. The common concern of caring for children of a similar age webbed together a relationship characterized by friendly conversations, neighborly niceties, and shared activities. Years later, when my wife's parents sold their home and moved away, one of the most poignant moments was their tearful good-bye with the evangelical Christian neighbors.

This is precisely the ethic that Jeffrey Stout speaks of in *Democracy and Tradition*, the "thick democratic practices" of conversation and activity across lines of difference that help to build a civic nation out of what might otherwise be a random gathering of people.[3] One can imagine a situation where these two households showed respect for one another's religious differences without the added dimension of warm relationship. It is certainly possible to accommodate someone's prayer practices yet refuse to let your kids play at their home. But it sure feels less inspiring.

Commitment to the Common Good

By common good, I mean the principles and structures of the broader entities we all live within, the "oneness of the community" that John Courtney Murray highlights. Committing to the common good means recognizing that our various identity expressions and relationships can only exist when those principles and structures are healthy. This refers to both highly concrete and extremely abstract matters. If the principle of free expression is eroded, all of our identities are threatened. If violent gangs roam the streets, getting to a PTA meeting where relationships between people who have different views on the Middle East can be built is more difficult. Simply put, the common good are those principles and structures that a range of groups benefit from and people generally agree we have a collective interest to uphold.

Of course, this all is made more complicated by the fact that people's identities shape their vision of the common good. People in favor of gay marriage speak about upholding the common good values of equal rights, dignity, and freedom. People opposed to gay marriage speak of the common good value of how marriage has been understood and practiced in Western civilization for centuries. But both views exist within a broader political community that allows free expression, civic and political associations, and an open legal system, and in a broader society with safe air travel, well-paved roads, and excellent communications systems. All identity communities have a stake in maintaining some version of the common good, some notion of the health of the whole.

One striking example of people with divergent views based on different identities finding common ground is the "You Stink" campaign in Lebanon.[4] Between 1975 and 1990, different religious groups waged a brutal civil war in that country, killing 120,000 people and forcing a million more to flee. The major political institutions are still deeply divided between religious groups, as is much of the social and economic life. In the summer of 2015, the various groups found something that brought them together. Trash was piling up across Beirut, creating an unpleasant smell and a health hazard. An organized effort called the "You Stink" campaign emerged. People from a range of religious communities put aside their divisions and animosities to gather together and peacefully demand that the trash be picked up. It is a potent example of how, even in a nation where diverse communities have a recent history of violence and deep current divisions, there are opportunities to identify and work toward some definition of the common good.

THE CIVIC GOODS OF INTERFAITH LEADERSHIP

The definition of pluralism is drawn largely from political philosophy. It is an attractive destination but, in keeping with the finest traditions of philosophy, a somewhat abstract one. Like the notion of "a more perfect union" in the Preamble to the US Constitution (another phrase from the pen of a political philosopher), it can be approached but never finally reached.

The upside here is that even heading in the direction of pluralism provides significant benefits, what I am calling the five civic goods of interfaith cooperation. These goods are derived from the social sciences, disciplines that generally seek more concrete outcomes than its cousin in the academy, political philosophy.

In continuing with our metaphor of building a bridge toward the destination of pluralism, it is reasonable to ask why anyone would take the time to build a bridge to a place that can never be arrived at. The answer is that the landscape becomes far more beautiful along the way. By moving toward the vision of pluralism, and building your bridge to reach that destination, you get to see the benefits of the following five civic goods:

1. *Increasing understanding and reducing prejudice.* Prejudice is the irrational dislike of certain identities, frequently race, gender, sexuality, disability, and/or religion. Prejudice is bad in a diverse society because it violates the dignity and rights of the target person or group, and also because it raises barriers to their contribution to the broader society. Contributions by citizens are the lifeblood of a democracy. Interfaith leadership facilitates the flow of contributions by increasing understanding of diverse identities and thereby reducing the barriers erected by prejudice.

2. *Strengthening social cohesion and reducing the chances for identity-based conflict.* I define "social cohesion" as the broad inclusion of people with different identities and positive relationships between them. Identity-based tensions and conflict are a significant problem in diverse societies. Social science evidence (see the discussion of Varshney in chapter 2) shows that social cohesion helps prevent such conflict. By accommodating diverse identity expressions, nurturing positive relationships between different communities, and upholding the broader community we all live within, interfaith cooperation strengthens social cohesion and also creates the conditions for bridging social capital.

3. *Bridging social capital and addressing social problems.* "Social capital" is generally defined as well-organized networks of

people whose energy is directed toward civic ends. Religious communities are the largest source of social capital in the United States. By bridging the social capital between diverse religious communities and channeling it toward a positive civic purpose, interfaith leaders have the opportunity to make a profound impact on social problems ranging from poverty to disease.

4. *Fostering the continuity of identity communities and reducing isolation.* We live at a time when identity communities across the board are losing members. While I am certainly not arguing for people to be forced to join or stay in communities against their will, Robert Putnam and David Campbell offer evidence that people who are part of such communities are both healthier and happier.[5] Moreover, such groups serve as the building blocks of social capital. Religious groups have long been one of the most important identity communities in the United States. Social scientists like Peter Berger and Christian Smith believe that an important reason for the erosion of such communities is because of the challenge they face in positively engaging diversity.[6] Interfaith leaders help faith and philosophical communities endure by providing them with a framework and language that helps them positively articulate their own identity in a diverse society, while at the same time building positive relationships with the various people around them.

5. *Creating binding narratives for diverse societies.* As mentioned earlier, in his paper "*E Pluribus Unum,*" Robert Putnam highlights the central role that grand narrative plays in binding together the various identities in a diverse nation.[7] The idea of America as an immigrant nation and the prominent place of *e pluribus unum* (out of many, one) on the Great Seal of the United States gives people of various backgrounds a sense of place and belonging in the United States. In "Civil Religion in America," the sociologist Robert Bellah highlights how religious symbols play an especially powerful role in such narratives.[8] Some of the most enduring images of the United States—Winthrop's "city on a hill," Lincoln's "almost chosen people,"

Addams's "cathedral of humanity," King's "beloved community"—have roots in religious texts and narratives. National symbols like the flag and the Pledge of Allegiance absorb some of these religious qualities. When used properly, these symbols can be utilized in a national narrative that communicates that the diversity within a nation is sacred and, thereby, ought to be cherished, protected, and positively engaged.

To be clear, these are not the *only* benefits associated with interfaith cooperation, just the most prominent civic goods. They fall under what might be called the "good neighbors" paradigm of interfaith work rather than the "fellow seekers" model, which highlights the more personal and spiritual dimensions of interfaith engagement. While the majority of this book emphasizes the civic rather than the personal, the good thing is that one does not have to give up the latter to gain the former. Indeed, as I explained in chapter 1, interfaith leadership is both a fulfilling personal journey and a way to make significant social impact.

THE INTERFAITH TRIANGLE

How does an interfaith leader know that she is building the bridge in the right direction, toward the destination of pluralism? This question brings up the thorny issue of how interfaith leaders measure their effectiveness at the same time they are running their programs.

There are at least two challenges with measuring the effectiveness of social programs. The first is accuracy. Measurement in social programs has to use proxies. The questions on an IQ test are a proxy for intelligence. The SAT exam is a proxy for how prepared a student is for college work. Neither of these is a perfect measure for the complex phenomenon that is intelligence or college readiness, but they are reasonable proxies, and the people who run them are constantly seeking to improve the instruments.

The second challenge in measuring the effectiveness of social programs is the burden involved. The evaluation effort should be reasonably easy to administer and analyze, and should definitely not take more time and energy than running the actual program. (The exception to this is when professional evaluators or academic researchers design a large-scale study intended to research one or more of the effects I've discussed.)

In creating an evaluation that is a reasonable proxy for the objectives I sketched out *and* that is easy to administer, it is useful to rely on the work of the experts. Social scientists measure America's religious diversity in three basic ways. The first and most common category is attitudes. This is a broad category, and there are many ways to ask questions about attitudes, but it generally comes down to a pretty basic sentiment: "Do you feel warmly toward Muslims, Jews, evangelicals, or humanists?" The second category is relationships. These are the "Do you know, work with, or have a friend from a different religion?" questions. The final category is knowledge. These are the "What religion is Shabbat associated with? In what faith do adherents fast from dawn to dusk for one month of the year?" types of questions.

The three measures are related, with an especially strong correlation between relationships and attitudes. Consider the following statistics. A 2007 Pew study found that 44 percent of people who *did not* know a Mormon had a positive attitude toward the Mormon community. Of those who *did* know a Mormon personally, *60 percent* had favorable views. That's a sixteen-point difference. The same question was asked regarding Muslims, and there the difference was even starker. Only 32 percent of people who *did not* know a Muslim expressed favorable views toward the community. But of those who *did* know a Muslim, 56 percent had positive attitudes. That's nearly a twenty-five-point difference.

In *American Grace*, Putnam and Campbell call this the "My Pal Al" principle, and explain it with this example: Say you are a beekeeper and your friend Al is a beekeeper. Apiculture brings you together, and through this shared activity, you learn that Al is an evangelical Christian. Prior to meeting Al, you harbored a host of prejudices about evangelicals, but if Al is a beekeeper and a good guy and an evangelical, then maybe other evangelicals aren't so bad. Putnam and Campbell actually show strong statistical evidence for this principle—that people's regard for entire religious groups improves through a positive, meaningful relationship with even one member of that group, often formed through a common activity.[9]

The data suggested something else as well: that by becoming friends with Al, the beekeeping evangelical, not only did your attitude toward evangelicals improve, so did your attitude toward Mormons and Muslims get better. Putnam and Campbell conclude: "We have reasonably firm evidence that as people build more religious bridges they become warmer toward people of many different religions, not just those religions represented within their social network."[10]

There is also evidence that knowledge of other traditions correlates with positive attitudes. A 2009 Pew study found that those who reported a high familiarity with Islam—for example, knowing that Muslims call God Allah and call their holy book the Qur'an—are three times more likely to have favorable views of Muslims than those who report low familiarity.[11] A Gallup survey released the same year found a similarly strong correlation between knowledge of Islam and attitudes toward Muslims.[12]

But it's not just any knowledge that matters; it's the type of knowledge that counts the most. Princeton University's Robert Wuthnow found that Americans regard Hindus, Buddhists, and Muslims as equally strange.[13] But twice the number of Americans say Muslims are fanatical. Why? Because the information they have on Muslims tends to be about extremist violence.

I think it is useful to view attitudes, knowledge, and relationships as three sides of a triangle, what I call the "interfaith triangle." If you know some (accurate and positive) things about a religion, and you know some people from that religion, you are far more likely to have positive attitudes toward that tradition and that community. The more favorable your attitude, the more open you will be to new relationships and additional appreciative knowledge.

The three sides of the interfaith triangle directly map onto the three parts of pluralism. Attitudes are a reasonable proxy for respect for identity, and knowledge is a decent proxy for understanding. Taken together, they can be viewed as measuring the absence of overt prejudice and the presence of positive understanding, the first of the five civic goods of interfaith cooperation. Relationships are a direct measure for, obviously, relationships.

But how can an interfaith leader measure more sophisticated civic goods, like social capital and social cohesion? To get at the answer to this question, it is useful to view the interfaith triangle as something people cycle around. As the attitudes-relationships-knowledge virtuous cycle gains steam, initiatives like interfaith service projects and mosque-synagogue-church exchanges become more widespread. This grows social capital, strengthens social cohesion, encourages people to remain within identity communities, and gives people a deeper appreciation for a national narrative that highlights the holiness of religious diversity.

The interfaith triangle is meant to be a reasonably accurate and easy-to-use evaluation model for interfaith leaders. Once you know that appreciative knowledge and meaningful relationships are connected to positive attitudes in the shape of an interfaith triangle, and that attaining a virtuous cycle around the interfaith triangle helps us achieve the higher-level objectives, you can design programs to maximize for knowledge and relationships. And you can create easy-to-analyze surveys that you administer to program participants, asking if they learned something that inspired them about a different religion or if they met someone they admired from another community. When respondents answer with an emphatic yes, your bridge is probably heading in the right direction. If they don't, then you might need to change some things.

CONCLUSION—OF MOUNTAINS AND ELEPHANTS

In concluding, I want to return to some of the themes I raised at the beginning of this chapter regarding religious diversity being about gathering people who disagree on ultimate concerns. It is impossible to overstate how real, and how challenging, this is. To return to the mountain metaphor, the climber should not be surprised that the mountain is present, but she is certainly justified in looking at it up close and personal and feeling daunted.

Because interfaith programs are often wrapped in a kind of feel-good gauziness, when the mountain of disagreement finally shows itself, it can seem especially rocky. I remember moderating a panel with two students at Alvernia University, one an atheist and the other a Catholic, who proudly proclaimed to an audience of their fellow students that their religious difference meant very little. They had the same politics, viewed social issues in similar ways, even liked the same music. Their message seemed to be that religious differences don't have to be scary because they don't mean all that much. Toward the end of the discussion, the atheist made an offhand comment that if he ever had children, he would be sure to expose them to all religions and philosophies, instead of just raising them in one. That, he said, was tantamount to child abuse. The young Catholic woman sitting to his left, who needless to say had been raised for her whole life as a Catholic and likely planned to raise her children in the same way, looked like she had seen a ghost. The pretense that different orientations around religion had no consequential implications collapsed just like that, in a moment of supreme discomfort.

One result of the presence of deep disagreements is a strong temptation to form interfaith coalitions around particular political and theological positions. Because of the primacy of polarizing politics in our era, there are many people who will jump at the chance to circle religiously diverse wagons around support for Israel or opposition to it, support for abortion or opposition to it, support for same-sex marriage or opposition to it. The list goes on. This is important organizing work in a diverse democracy, but interfaith leaders should be very careful about widening existing divides. The purpose of interfaith work is to build stronger connections between people who orient around religion differently. As political polarizations linked to faith commitments are among the most salient divisions of our time, interfaith leaders, in my view, ought to be highly concerned with seeking to narrow those divides rather than expand them.

A second challenge posed by deep disagreements is the inclination to focus only on the disagreement, to go right to the elephant in the room. That, in my experience, is not a good idea. When people charge toward the elephant, they instinctively bring out the spears they have been sharpening for years. They launch their weapons at high velocity, aim for the most sensitive places, and erect impenetrable defenses. It is almost impossible to turn people toward shared values and common ground once the war paint has gone on.

When people ask you why you are avoiding the elephant in the room, tell them it's because there are other animals in the zoo.

WiSdOm

KNOWLEDGE BASE

In the first four chapters, I have described what it takes to adopt the identity of interfaith leader, to acquire an understanding of the theoretical landscape on which you build your interfaith bridge, and to ensure that the bridge leads to the destination of pluralism. In the following chapter, I will discuss the various types of stones that serve as the raw materials for the bridge. Stones, of course, are a metaphor for knowledge. What I provide is a framework for the dimensions of knowledge most useful for forming an interfaith bridge.

FIVE

The Knowledge Base of Interfaith Leadership

Paul Knitter felt the call to the priesthood in his early teens. After four years of seminary high school and two years of additional novitiate training, he joined the Divine Word Missionaries (or SVD), an order whose main work was bringing non-Catholics into the Catholic faith. His regular prayers included the line "May the darkness of sin and the night of heathenism vanish before the light of the Word and the Spirit of grace."

Reflecting on this practice in his book *One Earth Many Religions*, Knitter writes, "*We* had the Word and Spirit; *they* had sin and heathenism. We were the loving doctors; they were the suffering patients."[1]

Knitter's journey took a number of unexpected turns. As he sat with the other seminarians listening to the stories of returned SVD missionaries, he discovered that he was fascinated by the slide shows of Hindu rituals and Buddhist ceremonies. He even detected a hint of admiration in the voices of older SVD priests as they described the elaborate non-Christian religious systems that they encountered on their missions. One brought in an Indian dance group and explained that their performance was developed in a Hindu context but had been adapted to glorify Jesus. Knitter was entranced by the intricacy of the movements and found himself wondering whether "sin and heathenism" were the most suitable terms for a tradition that could inspire such beauty. His explorations of Zen Buddhism, which he studied in preparation for evangelizing in Japan, produced much the same effect. He describes feeling deeply moved by "the rigor of its practice, the claimed illumination and peace of the satori experience. There was much I couldn't fit into my Christian categories; there was much I liked."[2]

In 1962, Knitter's studies took him to the Pontifical Gregorian University in Rome. He arrived just as the Second Vatican Council was getting under way. As the church conducted its business in Latin, and as Knitter's language skills were markedly better than many of the bishops who were a formal part of the council, he was asked to translate *sub secreto* (confidential) church documents by sheepish bishops on a nightly basis. One of these documents was the "Declaration on the Relationship of the Church to Non-Christian Religions," *Nostra Aetate*. Knitter was ecstatic to read the "positive statements about the truth and values" of religions like Hinduism, Buddhism, and Islam in an official church document.[3]

At the Gregorian, Knitter had begun studying with the renowned Jesuit theologian Karl Rahner, who was struggling to articulate the relationship between his notion of Christian uniqueness and his respect for other religions. Knitter would go on to do his doctorate on a related subject and begin dialogues with important Christian theologians like Hans Küng and John Hick on Christian approaches to other religions. Taken together, these turns set Knitter on the path to developing his own theology of interfaith cooperation, a path that would ultimately become his calling and profession.

In 1991, Knitter took a sabbatical year in India. There he discovered a history of both interfaith strife and interfaith cooperation. He spent time with Christian communities that had a long tradition of deep dialogue with Hindu, Muslim, and Buddhist groups focused on the goal of relieving suffering. He was inspired by the legacy of Gandhi's interfaith efforts, especially his focus on identifying nonviolence as a shared value across different religions and applying the techniques of creative nonviolence to improve social conditions. Knitter returned home with new energy and insight, even more committed to strengthening interfaith relations.

Paul Knitter's biography serves as a perfect case study in how a personal journey can lead to acquiring a knowledge base for interfaith cooperation. Indeed, the major turns of his story highlight the four dimensions of the knowledge base that I detail in this chapter. As a young man in training for the Catholic priesthood, Knitter encounters dimensions of Buddhism and Hinduism, and develops an *appreciative knowledge* for both. As a slightly older graduate student, he has an opportunity to study Christian *theologies of interfaith cooperation.* This opportunity happens to coincide with a remarkable moment in modern religious history, the deliberations of Vatican II and the release of *Nostra Aetate.* Later, and now in the role of professor, Knitter travels to India and comes face-to-face with the realities of religious conflict in the past but also an inspiring *history of interfaith cooperation.* He is especially struck by the power, exemplified by Gandhi, of *identifying shared values across traditions* and applying these to social action.

I highlight Knitter's personal journey to emphasize the idea that acquiring a knowledge base for interfaith cooperation need not be a dry or boring process. In fact, my guess is that your own personal journey has turned up some of these same four parts of an interfaith knowledge base, though perhaps without the drama of translating early drafts of *Nostra Aetate* for Latin-challenged bishops during Vatican II.

In this chapter, I will elaborate on each of these four dimensions— appreciative knowledge of other traditions, theology of religious pluralism, history of interfaith cooperation, and shared values between traditions. In the metaphor of the bridge, these various dimensions of knowledge serve as different types of stones for the bridge.

APPRECIATIVE KNOWLEDGE

In his award-winning book *Religious Literacy*, Stephen Prothero explores an interesting paradox in American life: Americans are highly religious but have little content knowledge about religious traditions—their own or those of others.[4] Prothero proves his case with myriad examples, including reporting on the depressing results of the religious literacy quizzes that he gives to his undergraduate students at Boston University. Such deep ignorance, he claims, is dangerous in a country like the United States, where public and political life is replete with religious topics and references. Prothero's proposed solution is to require that all students take two religion courses, one on the Bible and one on world religions. He reminds us that the Supreme Court has affirmed on several occasions—from the 1963 *Abington School District v. Schempp* case to *Edwards v. Aguillard* in 1987—that while the teaching *of* religion in public schools is unconstitutional, teaching a*bout* religion is both legal and important.

For such a program to be successful, Prothero cautions that it needs to be neutral in its approach. He writes, "Teachers should stick to describing and analyzing these religious traditions as objectively as possible, leaving it up to students to make judgments about the virtues and vices of any one religion, or of religion in general."[5]

I understand the reason for Prothero's counseling a "neutral" approach, not least because we are friends and have talked about this many times in person. Prothero hopes for a sea change in American education and is concerned that either the secular left or the religious right will seize on any kind of teaching about religion initiative as too preachy (in the case of the secular left) or too relativistic (in the case of the religious right). For Prothero, the only chance to chart a course in between this Scylla and Charybdis is to advocate an objective, neutral, "just the basics" approach.

I certainly think it would be an improvement on the status quo if more Americans could, for example, identify the Qur'an as the sacred scripture of Islam and locate nirvana as a Buddhist concept. But I do not think a just-the-basics understanding of other religions is a sufficient knowledge base for interfaith leaders. This is something I have hashed out with Prothero, and which he has not only agreed with but helped me come to better understand.

The main reason for this is that interfaith leaders are not dealing with abstract systems in textbooks, but actual people interacting in real-world situations. The renowned preacher Barbara Brown Taylor has a funny story about the difference. Teaching world religions at a small college in Piedmont, Georgia, she patiently reviewed the textbook's explanation of the doctrinal differences between Shia and Sunni Muslims, and tried to help her class of mostly rural, evangelical Christians see how those divisions could explain the violent intrafaith conflicts between Muslims they were accustomed to seeing on the news. Someone in the class turned to the lone Muslim student, a young man named Muhammad from Sierra Leone, and asked, "Are you a Sunni or a Shia? Do *you* hate the people on the other side?"

"I've never heard those words until today," he responded.

Certainly the terms "Sunni" and "Shia" would belong on a religious literacy quiz as an objective, neutral fact about Islam. But it was not an especially relevant bit of knowledge in that particular interfaith situation in Piedmont, Georgia.

My view is that interfaith leaders need what I am calling an "appreciative knowledge" of other traditions. By appreciative, I mean both a general orientation and a substantive knowledge base. As in the appreciative inquiry method of organizational development and the asset-based approach to community development, an appreciative orientation to other religious traditions actively seeks out the beautiful, the admirable, and the life giving rather than the deficits, the problems, and the ugliness. It is an orientation that does not take its knowledge about other religions primarily from the evening news, recognizing that, by definition, the evening news reports only the bad stuff. This is not to say that stories about terrorist attacks by Muslims, land grabs by Israeli settlers, or sexual misconduct by Catholic priests are false, only that they are not the whole truth. By being attuned to the inspiring dimensions of other religious traditions, such ugliness is properly contextualized. This general orientation is connected to an important skill that I will discuss in the next chapter—developing an interfaith radar screen.

The substantive dimension of appreciative knowledge has three main parts: recognizing the contributions of other traditions, having a sympathetic understanding of the distinctive history and commitments of other traditions, and developing ways of working with and serving other communities.

- The first part of an appreciative knowledge of other traditions is to recognize their contributions. In my experience, this is most effectively done through highlighting exemplary figures. This is the approach that Black History Month takes through a public registering and celebration of the contributions of major black figures, including writers, musicians, activists, and scientists. Initiatives like Black History Month do not focus only on neutral, objective facts, like the percentage of the US population that is black. The emphasis is instead to correct for a gap in the general knowledge base about underrepresented populations. Building an appreciative knowledge of the contributions of religious communities would take the same approach based on a similar rationale.

  An appreciative knowledge base about Islam would, for example, highlight that some of America's greatest athletes have been Muslim, including Muhammad Ali and Hakeem Olajuwan. It would recognize that Muslims like Rumi and Hafiz are among the best-selling poets in the United States, that a Muslim (Fazlur Rahman Khan) designed the Sears (now Willis) Tower in Chicago, and that a Muslim woman (Malala Yousafzai) is the youngest ever recipient of the Nobel Peace Prize. Ideally, these figures would be understood as illustrative of core Muslim principles like courage, commitment to excellence, and a high value on education.

- The second part of an appreciative knowledge base is developing a sympathetic understanding of where a differing religious view is coming from. For me, this is most powerfully illustrated in Chaim Potok's beautiful novel *The Chosen*, about the friendship between two Brooklyn-based Orthodox Jewish boys and their rabbi fathers at the end of World War II.[6] Danny's father, Reb Saunders, is a Hasidic rabbi who lives in a narrow world sealed off from other forms of knowledge and types of people. He is a perfect illustration of the bunker approach to diversity described in chapter 2. Reuven's father, Rabbi Malter, is of a more liberal bent and writes articles that put Judaism in conversation with other intellectual traditions and seek to make the tradition relevant to the contemporary world. He exemplifies the bridge response to diversity.

Reuven becomes a regular visitor to Danny's house and is taken aback by how Danny's father, Reb Saunders, treats his children and runs his community. Reuven learns, for example, that Danny's pretty teenage sister was promised to the son of one of Reb Saunders's followers when she was two years old. She will marry him when she turns eighteen. This is common Hasidic practice, Danny informs him. In fact, Danny's own marriage has been prearranged as well.

Danny and his father have no semblance of normal conversation at all. No words of affection, no simple banter about school or life or sports. The only time they communicate is on Friday evenings when Reb Saunders quizzes Danny in a harsh and unforgiving manner about Talmud and other dimensions of the Jewish tradition in front of the congregation that has gathered for the Shabbat service. Reuven comes to learn that, except for this weekly public spectacle, Reb Saunders is intentionally raising Danny in silence.

Reuven, who has a close relationship with his own father, is bewildered by Reb Saunders's behavior. He views it as cruel. Rabbi Malter, Reuven's father, also doesn't like Reb Saunders's interpretation of Judaism, but he understands where it comes from and takes the time to share the history with Reuven.

Reb Saunders, he explains, is a *tzaddik*, a righteous one. *Tzaddiks* personally led their people out of anti-Semitic Europe and into the relative safety of the United States with the primary purpose of creating communities to continue their Hasidic traditions. As a *tzaddik*, Reb Saunders believed it was his spiritual calling to personally absorb the suffering of his particular religious community, even the whole of Jewry. Rabbi Malter explains, "Reb Saunders is a great man, Reuven. Great men are always difficult to understand. He carries the burden of many people on his shoulders."[7]

The final part of the novel brings to light the full horror of the Holocaust—six million Jews killed in gruesome fashion—and causes a massive rupture between Reb Saunders and Reuven's father. Reb Saunders believes that the Holocaust is the will and work of God. The lot of Jews is to accept their suffering and to pray harder. Reuven's father sharply disagrees. For him, the story of the Holocaust is the story of the deeds of people, actions that other people can stop. The paramount action to take now is establishing a Jewish state, Israel. Rabbi Malter throws himself into this work with all of his energy. Reb Saunders views this as an apostate position. He believes that such a state can only legitimately be established at the time the Messiah returns. When Reb Saunders finds out about Reuven's father's advocacy for Israel, he explodes at Reuven and bans Danny from seeing him.

Even then, Reuven's father continues to articulate an appreciative understanding of Reb Saunders's position. "The fanaticism of men like Reb Saunders kept us alive for two thousand years of exile," he solemnly informs his son.[8] He does not hide his disagreements with Reb Saunders but remains restrained in his critique, saying, "There is enough to dislike about Hasidism without exaggerating its faults."[9] And when he reaches the limits of his own understanding of Reb Saunders's behavior, he simply tells Reuven, "I am not a *tzaddik*," emphasizing that Reb Saunders has made commitments to God, tradition, community, and family that put him in a different position, one that can be disagreed with but ought to be appreciated as well.[10]

The themes in *The Chosen* bear a striking resemblance to contemporary interfaith relations. What if a pro-Palestinian

Muslim could look at a pro-Israel Reform Jew and think, "I do not agree with her view, and I will protest and vote against it. But given the history of her people and her commitment to a particular tradition, I understand why she stands where she does. My position is also, after all, a function of my particular commitments to tradition and community." What if that pro-Israel Reform Jew, a strong supporter of abortion rights, could look at a Catholic priest who runs a school in the inner city and protests vehemently against abortion and think, "I will challenge him on his views regarding abortion, but I admire so much the work he does in education."

- The third part of an appreciative knowledge of other traditions is the kind of knowledge that allows you to work effectively with a different community. In her masterful book, *The Spirit Catches You and You Fall Down*, the writer Anne Fadiman tells the harrowing story of the Lees, a Hmong family in Merced, California, whose infant daughter Lia has suddenly begun to experience periodic convulsions.[11] The medical professionals at the state-of-the-art hospital, some of whom are widely regarded in their field, diagnose the condition as an electrochemical storm caused by the misfiring of brain cells, a condition commonly known in the West as epilepsy. They treat it in the manner of Western medicine, by taking blood, running tests, and prescribing various cocktails of drugs.

Few of the forty or so medical professionals who attend to Lia over the next few years have anything but the vaguest idea how her Hmong family and community understand her situation. Next to the religion box on a bureaucratic form, one has marked, *none*.

The Hmong believe that Lia's soul has been captured by a malevolent spirit called a *dab*. This occurred when Lia's older sister slammed a door too loudly, causing Lia's spirit to be frightened and run away, and a *dab* to take advantage of the opportunity. For Lia to get well again, her soul must be found and returned to her body. To accomplish this, chickens, pigs, and cows have to be sacrificed and a Hmong shaman must travel between the material world and spirit world to barter the souls of these ritually sacrificed animals for Lia's soul.

There is an interesting complication at the heart of the story. While Lia's physical shaking is certainly scary, the Lees believe that the situation is not all bad. The Hmong shamans that they call upon to serve as mediators between the material and the spirit worlds were often prepared for their roles by their own fits of uncontrollable shaking. This means that Lia's physical condition may be preparation for her ultimate role as a shaman as well, a revered position within the community. The Lees do not understand why the doctors seem to be oblivious to this sacred opportunity.

The doctors, for their part, are acutely frustrated that the Lees do not administer Lia's medicine properly. A senior doctor at the hospital decides at one point that the Lees are unfit as parents and has a California court put Lia into the care of the state for several months. It is a nightmare situation for any family, especially one that speaks no English and has a very limited understanding of the system.

The doctors, of course, see the Lees as noncompliant. They do not see the considerable effort the family is going through to care for their daughter according to Hmong shaman traditions. Many ceremonies have been held to coax Lia's soul back; many animals have been sacrificed; thousands of miles have been driven to consult with Hmong shamans in other parts of the country; expensive amulets have been purchased, filled with sacred healing herbs and carefully placed around Lia's neck.

After hundreds of seizures and dozens of trips to the hospital, Lia finally has the "big one" and is left in a vegetative state. It is a terrible situation. Fadiman cannot help but wonder whether things might have been different if the doctors had an appreciative understanding of Hmong religion. She offers the example of Dwight Conquergood as instructive.

Conquergood, an ethnographer with a special interest in shamanism and a performance artist with a creative flair, becomes a public health worker in a Hmong refugee camp in the 1980s. One of the first things he notices is a Hmong woman whose face is decorated with blue moons and golden suns. He recognizes them as the stickers that the Western doctors working in the camp were placing on medication bottles to indicate whether pills should be taken in the morning or at night. Clearly, they were not being used for their intended purpose. Conquergood notices that the woman is singing a folk song and wonders if the stickers decorating her body are somehow enhancing the drama of the song. It occurs to him that folk tales play a particularly powerful role in the Hmong worldview.

When an outbreak of rabies occurs among the dogs in the refugee camp, the medical staff attempts to organize a mass dog-vaccination program. Characteristically, they go about this in a manner that takes no account of Hmong worldview or religion. Not a single dog is brought to the medical facility. Conquergood is charged with creating a different campaign. Drawing on his observation of the power of folklore for the Hmong, Conquergood designs costumes for central figures in Hmong folktales—a tiger, a chicken, and a *dab*—and creates a drama in which these characters explain to the audience what rabies is and why it is dangerous. The next day, so many dogs were brought to the medical tent that the medical staff could not treat them quickly enough.

As specific as this situation might seem, some version of acquiring and creatively wielding knowledge of another community's faith is relevant across a vast number of settings and professions, from food preparation to funeral services.

THEOLOGIES OF INTERFAITH COOPERATION

A theology of interfaith cooperation means interpreting the key sources of a tradition in a way that puts forth a coherent narrative and deep logic that calls for positive relationships with people who orient around religion differently. When I say "key sources," I mean both the central texts of a religious tradition but also important historical moments, examples of archetypal figures, writings of significant scholars (philosophers, theologians, and jurists), and art that seeks to tap into the ineffable dimensions of the tradition. A coherent narrative is a theme that is clearly traceable throughout the different dimensions of a cumulative historical tradition (texts, history, archetypal figures, scholarship, and so on).

There are at least two reasons that developing such a theology is important for an interfaith leader. The first is personal. If you happen to be an interfaith leader who identifies deeply with a particular tradition—Christianity, Buddhism, humanism, and others—you will want to know at some point that your work as an interfaith leader is not in opposition to your tradition or ancillary to it, but rather expresses a central value of that tradition. In other words, being an interfaith leader is about advancing the five civic virtues I spoke of earlier, *and* it is part of being a faithful Jew, Sikh, Bahá'í, and so on. The renowned philosopher Alasdair MacIntyre expresses this sentiment well when he writes, "I can only tell you what I am going to do when I know the story or stories of which I am a part."[12] Those of us who view ourselves as part of religious traditions want our work in the world to be aligned with the "story" of our tradition. A theology of interfaith cooperation offers us the chance to develop an interpretation of that story. For atheists and humanists, the term "ethic" is probably more comfortable than "theology," but the principle of identifying a theme within the key sources of the tradition is much the same.

The second reason developing a theology of interfaith cooperation is important is for mobilizing *other people* who view themselves as connected to particular traditions. In his book *Why Did Jesus, Moses, the Buddha, and Mohammed Cross the Road?*, the Christian writer Brian McLaren notes that people generally believe that strong faith is connected with hostile views toward other communities. People with appreciative knowledge of other traditions and positive relationships with other communities consequently are viewed to have weak faith. This means that any time an interfaith leader proposes an interfaith activity to a group that thinks strong faith is a virtue, they are likely to think that such a path is meant to water down their faith. McLaren writes, "Many faithful Christians see our plea for them to become less hostile as a temptation to love God, their religion, their community, their ancestors, their history and their future less. Before they'll listen to our case for a new kind of strong-benevolent Christian identity, they must be convinced it is the path to more love and fidelity, more strength and meaning, not less."[13]

The solution to this problem is to define "strong faith" as including positive relationships with others and to offer interpretations of the tradition that substantiate this position. To do this, the interfaith leader is going to need to articulate a theology of interfaith cooperation.

My own Muslim theology of interfaith cooperation begins with important stories from the life of the Prophet Muhammad that speak to interfaith cooperation. In fact, the first people to recognize his prophethood were actually Christian: There was Bahira, a Christian monk who noticed that Muhammad, when he was a boy, had the mark of prophethood on his back. And there was Waraqa, who, after Muhammad's earth-shattering experience on Mount Hira in the year 610, explained to Muhammad and his wife Khadija that what Muhammad had experienced was God's revelation. The person most responsible for protecting Muhammad during the early years of Islam, when he and his fellow Muslims were hounded and harassed in Mecca, was a pagan, Abu Talib. One of Muhammad's first acts when he emigrated from Mecca to Medina was to create what became known as the Constitution of Medina, which allied the various religious groups and tribes in that area in an alliance of goodwill and common defense.

There are powerful moments from the classical period in Muslim history that affirm the value of interfaith cooperation, from the Prophet Muhammad inviting a group of Christians to pray in his mosque, to the Caliph Ali writing to his governor in Egypt: "All those there are your brothers in faith or your equals in creation."[14] Many Muslim groups since have followed in this tradition of respecting and protecting non-Muslims. The only country in Europe with a higher Jewish population *after* the Holocaust was Albania. The reason is that the people of that majority-Muslim country made it a part of their public honor to protect Jews during that dark time. Similarly, the Muslims of Rwanda appeared to be the only organized group who protected Tutsis from the machete-wielding Interahamwe militia during the genocide of the 1990s.

Like stories from the life of exemplary figures and key moments in history, religious art is an important contributor to a theology of interfaith cooperation. Muslim poets have long been known for their respectful attitudes toward other religions. Take Ibn Arabi, who wrote about his heart being capable of taking a range of religious forms, including a convent for Christians, a table for the Torah, and even a temple for idols.[15]

There are also key ideas in the Islamic tradition that can be interpreted as embracing of diversity. Take for example the term *ayat*, commonly understood as a "verse of the Qur'an," but more literally translated as "sign." God gives us his signs in many places—in his revealed scripture, in our relationships with others, in the natural world, and in the culture of the societies in which we live. In this way, the growing diversity of our societies may be viewed as an *ayat* of God and, therefore, something sacred.

For a tradition like Islam, the text is central. A theology of interfaith cooperation needs to involve the dimensions I've cited and also have an interpretation of the sacred scripture that supports and advances such a theology. In a brilliant essay entitled "The Place of Tolerance in Islam," the Islamic scholar Khaled Abou El Fadl accomplishes this task in a particularly audacious way. He lists various verses from the Qur'an that are clearly intolerant toward other religions alongside verses that command positive interfaith relationships and essentially asks, Why should we follow one set of verses rather than the other?[16]

The verses in question could not be more different. Here is an example on the intolerant side: "Fight those among the People of the Book who do not believe in God or the Hereafter, who do not forbid what God and His Prophet have forbidden, and who do not acknowledge the religion of truth—fight them until they pay the poll tax with willing submission and feel themselves subdued." (9:29)

And an example that calls for interfaith cooperation: "O human-kind, God has created you from male and female and made you into diverse nations and tribes so that you may come to know each other. Verily, the most honored of you in the sight of God is he who is the most righteous." (49)

Which view is the "correct" one? When it comes to relating with Christians and Jews, what should a conscientious Muslim do? To answer this question, Abou El Fadl puts forth a "hermeneutic" (a fancy word for "way of interpreting") for approaching the Qur'an that essentially has four parts. I will present these parts and augment Abou El Fadl's argument with the views of other Muslim scholars who also hold to a Muslim theology of interfaith cooperation.

The first part of the hermeneutic has to do with the historical context of the text. Muslims believe that the Qur'an was revealed over the course of twenty-three years, years during which the Prophet Muhammad was not only spreading the message of Islam but building a Muslim society. As in any real-world movement, there were moments of tension and conflict both within the fledgling Muslim community and between Muslims and other groups—Jews, Christians, Sabians, pagans—in the area. According to Muslim belief, God would reveal Qur'anic verses that helped the Prophet Muhammad deal with particular situations—this specific dispute between two people, that group over there causing problems. Many Muslim scholars, Abou El Fadl among them, say that the verses from the Qur'an that are intolerant toward other groups are meant to be specific advice for particular times and places, and not meant to be applied broadly. The verses that speak of interfaith cooperation, on the other hand, contain an ethic that is meant to be understood in a universal and eternal way.

The second part of the hermeneutic deals with the overall moral thrust of the Qur'an. Abou El Fadl points out that at the center of the Qur'an are a set of "general moral imperatives such as mercy, justice, kindness, or goodness" and that the entire text must be read "in light of the overall moral thrust of the Qur'anic message."[17] In his essay "Mercy: The Stamp of Creation," Dr. Umar Abd-Allah affirms this view and states that the core value of Islam is mercy. He writes, "Islamic revelation designates the Prophet Muhammad as 'the prophet of mercy,' and Islam's scriptural sources stress that mercy—above other divine attributes—is God's hallmark in creation and constitutes his primary relation to the world from its inception through eternity, in this world and the next."[18] Abd-Allah highlights what is known as the tradition of primacy in Islam, the first lesson that classical Muslim scholars taught their students: "People who show mercy to others will be shown mercy by the All-Merciful. Be merciful to those on earth, and he who is in heaven will be merciful to you."[19]

Third is the conscience of the reader. In addition to the historical context of the text and the general principles of the Qur'an, Abou El Fadl emphasizes that morality is contained not only in the text but also in the heart or conscience of the reader. After all, according to Muslim belief, God gave all people his breath (*ruh*). People are required to bring this inner morality to their reading of the Qur'an, and their lives in general. As Abou El Fadl writes, "The meaning of the religious text is not fixed simply by the literal meaning of its words, but depends, too, on the moral construction given to it by the reader . . . The text will morally enrich the reader, but only if the reader will morally enrich the text."[20] This particular view is probably most associated with Fazlur Rahman, among the twentieth century's most important Muslim scholars. In his book *Major Themes of the Qur'an*, Rahman writes that *taqwa*, translatable as "inner torch" or "moral conscience," is probably the most important single term in the Qur'an. It is the quality through which people align themselves with God's will.[21]

Finally, the context of the reader matters. Like all texts, the Qur'an emerges in a particular time and place. And like all people, we read it in particular times and places. In interpreting the Qur'an, both the context of the text and the context of the reader have to be taken into account. To support this view, Abou El Fadl gives the following example: "The Qur'an persistently commands Muslims to enjoin the good. The word used for 'the good' is ma'ruf, which means that which is commonly known to be good. Goodness, in the Qur'anic discourse, is part of what one may call a lived reality—it is the product of human experiences and constructed normative understandings."[22] In other words, the Qur'an expects readers to approach the text not only with their God-given *taqwa*, but also with ideas of what is "good" from their own context. For Abou El Fadl, this means that evolving notions in culture and civilization, from progress in science to ideals like universal human rights and the benefits of diversity, ought to be brought to bear when interpreting the Qur'an.

In his essay "Islam and Cultural Imperative," Dr. Umar Abd-Allah reinforces this view. He emphasizes that the genius of Islamic civilization was its ability to integrate its sacred law in various cultural contexts. In fact, he writes, one of the five maxims of Islamic law is to respect cultural usage and sound custom across time and place. Islam is meant to be a tradition that harmonizes with a range of cultures, not sets out to destroy them.[23] To support his point, he quotes from a renowned thirteenth-century Islamic legal scholar, Al-Qarafi: "Persons handing down legal judgments while adhering blindly to the texts in their books without regard for the cultural realities of their people are in gross error. They act in contradiction to established legal consensus and are guilty of iniquity and disobedience before God."[24]

At the end of his essay, Abou El Fadl emphasizes that any tradition, including Islam, "provides possibilities for meaning, not inevitabilities. And those possibilities are exploited, developed and ultimately determined by the reader's efforts."[25] No doubt one can understand the Qur'an and the Islamic tradition as one that compels building bunkers of isolation or barriers of division. One possibility does not, of course, mean the only possibility. One of the fascinating things about religious traditions is that they contain a multiplicity of potential interpretations and expressions. Some of these seem, at least from the outside, contradictory. Islam can be read as a religion that both seeks converts and emphasizes cooperation. The real question is not, therefore, "What does Islam say?" It is, "Which of the many possibilities and logics within Islam do I most want to emphasize?" That has as much to do with the reader's understanding of the tradition and the times as it does with anything else. What is crystal clear is that the tradition of Islam, like other major world traditions, has ample resources through which a faithful Muslim can construct a theology of interfaith cooperation.[26]

HISTORY OF INTERFAITH COOPERATION

I caught up with an old friend from high school one summer day a few years back. When I told her I was involved in interfaith work, she scoffed and said something to the effect of, "Religions have always fought, and they will always fight. End of story. At least that's what we learned in high school." It was true. What little education we got about religion in our high school was mostly related to violence—Islam spreading by the sword, the European wars of religion, the Spanish Inquisition, the Holocaust. Clearly, it shaped her framework.

Flipping through the *New York Times* later that day (July 12, 2013), I realized how high-profile current events seem to confirm my friend's paradigm. The picture on the cover was of a Bosnian Muslim mourning the Srebrenica massacre, where more than seven thousand Muslim men and boys had been executed on this day eighteen years earlier. In The Hague, genocide charges were reinstated against Radovan Karadžić, a wartime leader of the Bosnian Serbs, for his role in massacres against Bosnian Muslims during the 1992–1995 war in the Balkans. The Taliban, a Muslim extremist group in Afghanistan and Pakistan, were vowing to attack schools for girls, calling the education of women a Western plot against Islam. Officials in Northern Ireland were calling in police reinforcements in response to a rise in tensions between Catholics and Protestants. More than twenty Buddhists in Myanmar, many of them part of the extremist 969 movement, were given jail time because of their role in an attack on a Muslim school that killed thirty-six people. Members of the Muslim Brotherhood in Egypt were vocally denouncing the Christian minority in that country, claiming that Christians were responsible for the overthrow of Mohamed Morsi, the former president, who was closely aligned with their party. Closer to home, articles on abortion in North Carolina, gay marriage in Pennsylvania, the availability of "morning after" pills in New York City public schools, and federal immigration legislation all made reference to religious tensions.

My high school friend's conviction that religious diversity could only ever be associated with violence is a classic case of what scholars call *inference error*. Humans tend to make sweeping judgments based on two things—the knowledge structures (narratives, theories, schemas) we carry in our minds, and recent vivid instances that fit within the broader story of those knowledge structures. My friend's knowledge structure about religion was set in high school, through history lessons about the prominent role of religion in conflict. Viewing religion as an agent of violence across the span of history heightened her sensitivities toward stories in which religion is associated with violence today. The fact that the news is full of those stories simply confirmed her worldview.

Perhaps this is why so many people were so taken by Samuel Huntington's "clash of civilizations" theory. It was not so much an accurate appraisal of history as it was a compelling confirmation of people's psychological biases.

All of this made me think of one of the most profound moments in my life. It took place in Cape Town, South Africa, in December 1999, just before the turn of the millennium. I had gone there to help organize the youth program for the Parliament of the World's Religions, and I had gotten myself a ticket to hear Nelson Mandela speak.

When he came on stage, he looked even more regal than he had in the pictures I had seen of him. A man in the back stood and began to sing a chant that the person next to me explained was a praise song for an African chief. Mandela cocked his head to the side and closed his eyes and let the chant fill the room and wash over him. When it was over, he pointed out to the Cape in the direction of Robben Island and said, "I would still be there, where I spent a quarter century of my life, if it were not for the Muslims and the Christians, the Hindus and the Jews, the African traditionalists and the secular humanists, coming together to defeat Apartheid."

I was both inspired and stunned. Inspired because the image of people praying in different languages and working together to end a system of oppression gave me goose bumps. Stunned because, somehow, I had never considered this possibility before. Although I wasn't as set in a paradigm of religion-connected-to-conflict as my high school friend, I certainly did not have a clearly articulated knowledge structure regarding interfaith cooperation, or nearly enough compelling cases to form one.

In my view, an interfaith leader has to have both. Partially this is about having a more complete picture of history. As David Cannadine writes in his book *The Undivided Past*, "Open war has never been the whole picture in the history of religion, for alongside (and even during) periods of wrenching disagreements and searing spiritual conflicts, there have also been times of toleration and episodes of peaceful interaction."[27] Partially this is about forming a paradigm that gives us hope for the future. As Zachary Karabell writes in his book about the history of interfaith cooperation, *Peace Be Upon You*, "If we emphasize hate, scorn, war, and conquest, we are unlikely to perceive that any other path is viable."[28]

All of this is why interfaith leaders need a knowledge base that includes a history of interfaith cooperation.

In my mind, such a knowledge base recognizes that history doesn't simply happen; people make it. Consequently, the most powerful examples of interfaith history are cases where people have intentionally erected bridges of interfaith cooperation. Illustrations involving social movements—King and Rabbi Abraham Joshua Heschel in the Jim Crow South, Gandhi and Badshah Khan in colonial India—are undoubtedly inspiring. But lately I have been favoring cases that are not quite as well known, the behind-the-scenes interfaith movements that explain seemingly magical historical shifts.

In 1955, the sociologist Will Herberg wrote, "To be an American today means to be . . . a Protestant, a Catholic, or a Jew."[29] Just a quarter century earlier, there was a widespread sentiment that Catholics and Jews were not fully Americans. A Catholic candidate, Al Smith, had been trounced in the 1928 presidential election in a frenzy of religious prejudice. Catholics were viewed as aliens in America, undemocratic by nature and given to fascism. Jews were commonly portrayed as financially devious, clannish, and unwilling to assimilate. They were blamed for everything from the Great Depression in the United States to Hitler's rise in Europe. Both groups were commonly understood to be loyal to foreign elements rather than American democracy. The slogan of the Ku Klux Klan—"Native, white, Protestant supremacy"—described the conviction of a good part of America. Even Franklin Roosevelt privately said that the United States was "a Protestant country, and the Catholics and Jews are here under sufferance."[30]

So what accounts for the profound shift in attitudes regarding Catholics and Jews between the time of Al Smith's presidential campaign in 1928 and Herberg's book in 1955? The answer, according to social historian Kevin Schultz, lies in the work of an organization called the National Conference of Christians and Jews, commonly known as the NCCJ (which now stands for the National Conference for Community and Justice). Formally launched in 1928 to combat the growing popularity of the Klan, the NCCJ took as its mission the advancement of a tri-faith America where Protestants, Catholics, and Jews were understood as equally American, none suffered discrimination, and all worked closely together to benefit the common good. NCCJ programs quickly took root across the United States. One of the most popular was the Tolerance Trio—a Protestant minister, a Catholic priest, and a Jewish rabbi—who barnstormed across the country, engaging in "trialogue" with one another and giving presentations to religious and civic groups. These presentations inspired local tri-faith organizations in two hundred US cities and two thousand small towns.[31] When the United States entered World War II, in the early 1940s, NCCJ Tolerance Trios became a staple of military life. By the end of the war, they had spoken to nine million US servicemen and -women across nearly eight hundred military installations.[32] NCCJ films and printed materials reached even more. In the immediate aftermath of the war, the NCCJ partnered with the Ad Council to create the "United America" campaign, which promoted the tri-faith ideal on dozens of popular radio and television programs. The campaign lasted for six years, making over a billion audience impressions in 1949 alone.

In his review of the NCCJ's impact, the sociologist Alfred McClung Lee wrote that the organization's programs were creating "a social change with permanent effects."[33] Herberg's determination in *Protestant-Catholic-Jew* that all three of these communities were equally American affirmed McClung's findings.[34] Little is remembered today, in the popular imagination at least, of these highly intentional and effective efforts. People seem to have a faint recollection that there was once ugly bias against Catholics and Jews in American history, but such sentiments simply faded away as the nation evolved. It is closer to the truth to say that a group of people formed an organization that intentionally drove that prejudice into the past. To borrow an insight from Martin Luther King Jr.: It is a mistake to think that the pendulum of history swings of its own accord. The reality is, *people push it.*

Knowing interfaith history helps you understand how others have pushed that pendulum, and gives you the conviction that you might do it, too.

SHARED VALUES

Finally, I return to the biography and insights of Paul Knitter. As I wrote at the beginning of this chapter, Knitter's personal journey allowed him to acquire an appreciative knowledge of multiple religions, develop a theology of interfaith cooperation from his own Catholic faith, and learn about the history of interfaith cooperation in countries like India. Over the course of his life and career, Knitter used this vast knowledge base to identify shared values across traditions and to learn from the diverse ways that traditions approached such shared values.

For interfaith leaders, both shared values and diverse approaches are important. Religious and ethical traditions hold values like compassion, peace, and hospitality in common. But they approach these values in highly diverse ways, through different rituals, narratives, heroes, and philosophies. This is a hugely important opportunity for interfaith leaders because it gives us a way to identify *commonality without the pretense of sameness.* If Muslims, Hindus, and humanists all related the same story when you asked them to speak about hospitality, it would be like pointing to the same stone. The fact that they are likely to cite different texts and rituals when speaking about hospitality means that they are bringing diverse stones to the gathering.

Knitter's own story in this regard is especially striking. In his beautiful book *Without Buddha I Could Not Be a Christian*, he addresses how Christianity and Buddhism approach the shared value of peace in remarkably different ways.[35] In part inspired by his knowledge of the history of interfaith cooperation, and in part moved by Christian theological concepts like creating the kingdom of God on earth, Knitter becomes involved in social action organizations like Christians for Peace in El Salvador (CRISPAZ) and the Peace Council that seek to stop violence in various parts of the world. He travels with these organizations to El Salvador, Mexico, Israel, and elsewhere, often in interfaith groups, to promote peace. As part of his work, Knitter participates in protests against government forces and the upper class, writes papers on the "structural violence" of certain policies, and mobilizes people to action in American churches. He feels confident that he is engaging in a prophetic tradition of witnessing for justice—a central Christian idea in his interpretation of Christianity—but he also struggles. Is he really being effective, he wonders? Year after year, he sees more and more violence. Even as the number of demonstrators increases and the size of the protests grow, the reality on the ground is still more violence. He has to ask himself, Is this really the way to peace?

That is when he awakens to the very different approach that Buddhism takes to the shared value of peace. As he prepares once again to confront the death squads in El Salvador, a Zen master tells him, "You won't be able to stop the death squads until you realize your oneness with them."[36] As he sits with indigenous people in Chiapas, crafting a statement that denounces the North American Free Trade Agreement, he hears a Buddhist monk who is part of the Inter Religious Peace Council calmly desist, stating, "I'm sorry, but we Buddhists don't denounce anything."[37] As he participates in ceremonies to commemorate the horror of the Holocaust in Jerusalem, he observes a Buddhist monk ask, "But why do you have to remember? What would happen if you let go of such memories of suffering?"[38] The monk explained that in the Buddhist view, the Nazis were acting out their karma and deserved sympathy, just as the Chinese do for their persecution of Tibetans. To hold on to terrible memories is simply to relive the persecution, perhaps even to recycle the karma. The better course is detachment.

As Knitter deepens his exploration of Buddhist approaches to peace, he realizes just how different they are from Christian approaches. Prominent dimensions within Christianity emphasize the importance of action in the belief that the world is meant to head in a particular direction and Christians must accelerate the process. Peace comes when Christians bend the arc. Prominent dimensions within Buddhism emphasize contemplation, cultivating nonviolence within oneself. Knitter is shocked to discover that Buddhism does not really have a theology of justice. He is so used to the progressive Christian chant, "No justice, no peace," that he believes it to be a universal. But for Buddhists, to achieve peace, one must first *be* peace. Nor does Buddhism have a concept of the world heading in any particular direction, something that is central to Christian eschatology. In Buddhism, the universe is simply here, and Buddhists are meant to be mindfully here with it.

Ultimately, Knitter finds ways to connect these stones, the Christian approach to peace and the Buddhist one. He has long been confused by the Christian paradox of waiting for the kingdom of God and accelerating its arrival, what Christian theologians refer to as the "already/not yet" problem. The Buddhist equanimity about the natural tension between contemplation and action seems to be a useful parallel. He tells a Zen master that he feels the need both to meditate and to stop the death squads, and he cannot figure out which one he should pursue. The Zen master simply says, "They are both absolutely necessary. You have to sit. You have to stop the death squads." That Buddhist wisdom helps Knitter be present with the tension, recognizing it as simply a part of the nature of both the universe and the human condition. Energy devoted to disentangling the tension is wasted, a distraction from the important task of being mindfully present.

SKILL SET

The stones of interfaith knowledge do not magically form themselves into a bridge, much less one held together by an arch. The work of linking stones takes the interfaith skills that I outline in this next chapter. Sometimes, interfaith leaders will use the skill of public narrative to connect stones that they themselves have collected by using their interfaith radar screen. Sometimes they will curate an interfaith activity and facilitate an interfaith discussion to evoke stones of interfaith knowledge from the group. To create an arch, meaning a shape that ensures the bridge to pluralism holds, interfaith leaders have to take great care in connecting different stones in proper ways. Which stone of theology connects best with what stone representing a shared value? Finally, an interfaith leader will need the skills of relationship building and mobilizing to gather a group in the first place. After all, what is the use of building a bridge toward pluralism if you haven't gathered a group willing to take the journey?

SIX

The Skill Set of Interfaith Leadership

Here are the five key skills for interfaith leadership:

1. Building a radar screen for religious diversity
2. Developing a public narrative of interfaith cooperation
3. Building relationships and mobilizing religiously diverse constituencies
4. Creating activities that bring together people who orient around religion differently
5. Facilitating interfaith conversations with a religiously diverse group

A RADAR SCREEN FOR RELIGIOUS DIVERSITY

Over the last fifty years, diversity issues have become more prominent in American life and discourse. We talk about communities of color and the police, the gender gap in the corporate boardroom, and the marginalizing effects of heterosexism. There is a general awareness and an emerging language for race, gender, and sexuality issues in our culture.

We pay attention to these parts of identity; they register when we see them. In other words, we have a radar screen for these dimensions of diversity. Interfaith leaders need to develop the same kind of radar screen for religious diversity issues. The absence of such a radar screen has created problems from the highest reaches of the US government to the quads of American college campuses.

In 2006, Madeleine Albright wrote a book called *The Mighty and the Almighty* that lamented the State Department's absence of interfaith expertise during her years as secretary of state in the Clinton administration. The book amounted to an admission of paradigm failure on the part of the United States foreign policy elite. Albright writes, "We had in mind a future in which nations and regions drew closer as democratic bonds grew stronger, not a world splitting apart along historic fault lines of culture and creed."[1] Consequently, the State Department had legions of economic experts, but only a single person charged with understanding interfaith dynamics. This left the United States woefully unprepared to engage the religious energies at the heart of the conflicts in the Middle East, the Balkans, Northern Ireland, South Asia, and parts of Africa. What might have happened if there had been a more developed radar screen for religious diversity at the State Department? A two-state agreement between Israel and the Palestinians is one of several possibilities Albright dangles.

The foreign policy establishment is far from the only place where a radar screen for religious diversity is relevant. When I was a campus leader at the University of Illinois in the 1990s, we received significant training on identity issues. We discussed studies and did exercises on how people of different races are treated, everywhere from department stores to police stations, and how such experiences might color their perspective on a range of issues. When O. J. Simpson went on trial for murder, campus leaders at the University of Illinois were prepared for how black students and white students might view the trial differently. We organized discussion forums and educational programs that helped bridge the perspective gap both before and after the verdict. Our radar screen for racial diversity was reasonably well developed, and it helped us recognize possible tensions in our community even before they emerged.

When Mel Gibson's film *The Passion of the Christ* was released in 2004, with a storyline that many Christians viewed as honoring their faith but with character depictions offensive to many Jews, tensions between those two communities erupted at the University of Illinois. Student leaders told me that such animosity came as a surprise to people across campus. They neither anticipated it, nor had a good sense for how to manage it going forward. While they had all been trained on other identity issues, there had been no talk of religious identity in any of their leadership workshops. They had no radar screen for interfaith issues and, therefore, no way to prepare for the conflict that exploded in their faces.

If you were an airplane, you would simply install the necessary up-grades to your radar system. But since you are a person, you have to view the development of a radar screen for religious diversity as a skill similar to the other skills discussed in this chapter. Like learning how to mobilize religiously diverse people or facilitating a conversation among them, it is something to be worked at and improved. I list developing an interfaith radar screen as the first skill because I think it is foundational to the others. It is hard to curate activities for people who orient around religion differently or facilitate an interfaith dialogue if you are failing to register patterns of religious difference.

I want to highlight four related parts to the radar screen: immediate situations, current events, long-term trends, and the appreciative knowledge mentioned in the previous chapter.

By "immediate situations," I mean the religious diversity that is present in the civic spaces you normally inhabit. If you are a teacher in a religiously diverse school, how might the month of Ramadan affect Muslims? A sophisticated interfaith radar screen would recognize not only the obvious (fasting Muslims might want to go somewhere other than the cafeteria for lunch), but also the more subtle implications. Ramadan might be "outing" some students as Muslim, students who otherwise keep their religion under wraps because they are afraid of being bullied on account of their faith. A teacher with an interfaith radar screen would consider ways of addressing this issue long before the first day of Ramadan.

The second part of an interfaith radar screen is being attuned to the religious energies of relevant current events. I am a daily reader of the *New York Times*, and part of my personal commitment to strengthening my interfaith radar screen is to mentally mark every article I read that has interfaith implications and do the intellectual exercise of connecting those current events to the civic spaces I commonly inhabit. What new conversations and conflicts might the recent Supreme Court ruling guaranteeing same-sex marriage catalyze in the more conservative Christian colleges where I work?

The third part of an interfaith radar screen is keeping up with long-term trends in religion. My own practice is to regularly review surveys done by Pew, Gallup, and the Public Religion Research Institute (PRRI), read analyses written by scholars like Martin Marty and Robert Jones, and familiarize myself with the major books written in the field of public religion. And, as with my reading of current events, I am constantly seeking to connect long-term trends with the concrete work I do in civic spaces. For example, in his most recent book, *The End of White Christian America*, Robert Jones highlights how three significant trends will reshape the religious landscape in the United States: diversity, disaffiliation, and division.[2] There are many questions that these trends ought to raise for interfaith leaders. What new interfaith conflicts and alliances might emerge from the growing diversity of the American religious landscape? How does the trend toward disaffiliation from religious community affect social capital in America?

The final part of an effective interfaith radar screen is being attuned to the type of knowledge I wrote about in the previous chapter. Appreciative knowledge of other traditions, a theology of interfaith cooperation, a working knowledge of the history of interfaith cooperation, and shared faith values are not acquired in one fell swoop but accumulated over time by paying attention to these things, having a radar screen for them. It's like being a kid on a beach hunting for smooth stones, the ones that skip well over the water. Interfaith leaders should always be on the lookout for the stones of the interfaith knowledge base.

PUBLIC NARRATIVE

The idea of leadership as changing a public narrative is at the root of Howard Gardner's classic book in leadership studies, *Leading Minds*. The thesis of the book is strikingly simple: the defining quality of an effective leader is the ability to relate an influential story to the world and embody that story in your life. Gardner emphasizes that he chooses the word "story" over the word "message": "In speaking of stories, I want to call attention to the fact that leaders present a dynamic perspective to their followers: not just a headline or snapshot, but a drama that unfolds over time, in which they—leader and followers—are the principal characters or heroes."[3] Similarly, Gardner does not use the verb "tell" when he speaks of how leaders communicate stories; he uses the word "relate." Just as "story" is more dynamic than "message," "relate" is richer than "tell."

What does it mean to effectively relate an interfaith story? The first requirement is to be aware of the stories you are competing against. The most common competing narrative that interfaith leaders face is that religious diversity inevitably becomes barriers and bludgeons. The sum total of these smaller stories, told day after day on media platform after media platform, is a larger story about the role religious diversity plays in the world. The goal of an interfaith leader is to lift up the possibility of bridges of cooperation to a world increasingly convinced that religious diversity leads inevitably to barriers and bludgeons.

Marshall Ganz, professor at Harvard and a veteran of the civil rights movement, says that there are three types of public stories that leaders must master: stories of self, us, and now. A story of self is a story of calling, why *you* have chosen a particular line of work or identity category. It is the public relating of your narrative identity (see chapter 1). Note the resonance here with Ricoeur's "Here I am." Ganz emphasizes that leaders *must* tell their stories of self. If you do not own and tell your story, you leave a vacuum for others to conjure their own interpretations for your actions and leadership. People who oppose the change you seek to make will pounce on this opportunity and exploit it. In addition to guarding against negative interpretations, stories of self inspire others. As Ganz writes, "You have to claim authorship of your story and learn to tell it to others so they can understand the values that move you to act, because it might move them to act as well . . . all of us walk around with a text from which to teach, the text of our own lives."[4]

It is important to note that relating your own leadership story publicly is not the same thing as opening up your diary for the world to read. A public leadership narrative of self is selective and strategic, meant to give others a window into your motivation for being a particular type of leader and inspire them to reflect on their motivations for being part of the work. Its purpose is not primarily confessional. Its purpose is to motivate others to action.

A story of us is a story of a community with a purpose. A community is more than a group of people who happen to randomly share something. Just because you live on the same block with other people or work in the same company does not make that group of people a community or even give them a palpable sense of common purpose. We build community and purpose through the stories we share with one another, and the story we tell about the entire group. As Ganz writes, "We've all been in places where people have worked together for years, but there's no us there because they don't share their stories."

How do we build a sense of us? What kind of stories do we tell to each other and about our group? Ganz specifies: stories about the values and experiences we share, the hope and fear we harbor, the history we look back upon, and what we wish for the future. The important thing for the purpose of building a sense of us, Ganz emphasizes, is "putting what we share into words." In other words, relating stories.

The final type of story that leaders relate, according to Ganz, is stories of "the fierce urgency of now." Stories of now begin with the recognition that there is a gap between the values the community cherishes and the values by which the world operates. Ganz writes, "We need to appreciate the challenge and the conflict between the values by which we wish the world lived and the values by which it actually does. The difference between those two creates tension. It forces upon us consideration of a choice. What do we do about that?"

Stories of now move into answering that choice with a plan of action, a plan that will move the world closer to operating by the values that the community cherishes. Ganz emphasizes that stories of now cannot only emphasize the negative. Instead, stories of now must emphasize hope. Stories of now trade on the idea that this moment presents us with a unique opportunity to make progress, to close the gap, to nudge the world toward operating upon the values we cherish.

In addition to setting out the self-us-now framework in his *Sojourners* piece, Ganz offers a personal illustration. He begins the article with the story of self, recounting childhood stories of Passover seders in his home in Bakersfield, California, where his father was a rabbi and his mother a teacher. He writes, "There's a part in the Passover Seder when they point to the kids and say, 'You were a slave in Egypt.' I finally realized the point was to recognize that we were all slaves in Egypt and in our time the same struggle from slavery to freedom is always going on, that you have to choose where you stand in that." Those memories caused him to leave Harvard, where he was an undergraduate student, and go to Mississippi to become an organizer in the civil rights movement. That is Ganz's story of self—his public interpretation of his personal story about becoming a civil rights leader.

The story of us that Ganz tells is about the other young people who were leaving college or jobs or the normal habits of their lives to join the civil rights movement: "I went to Mississippi because it was a movement of young people, and there's something very particular about young people. . . . Young people come of age with a critical eye and a hopeful heart." There are several stories of "us" that Ganz could have highlighted in this piece—the "us" of rich and poor, of black and white, of farm workers and farm owners. Why emphasize the "us" of young people in this piece? Perhaps because he is now a college professor seeking to motivate a new generation of young people to view themselves as a community engaged in critical social change.

For the story of now, Ganz points to the inequalities he saw between blacks and whites in the South, and the hope he saw in the 1955 Montgomery bus boycott. The horrors of segregation represented for him the gap between the values of his community (young people) and the reality of the world. The success of the Montgomery bus boycott offered a plan of action (proactive peaceful protest) and hope that it would move the world closer to the community's values. Witnessing all of this as a Harvard undergraduate in 1960, Ganz felt a palpable choice and responded by leaving Harvard to participate in the civil rights movement in Mississippi.

I could not help but notice the interfaith themes in Ganz's article, no doubt an illustration of my own overactive interfaith radar screen. Ganz's own story of self begins with memories of Passover seders when he was a child, and the model of his rabbi father who had worked with Holocaust survivors. Ganz quotes from influential Christian figures like Paul Tillich and Walter Brueggemann, and cites the example of Gandhi's *satyagraha* movement. He frequently calls upon stories from Jewish, Christian, and Hindu traditions. For me, it is an excellent illustration of the frequency with which interfaith themes are present in leadership narratives of all types.

BUILDING RELATIONSHIPS AND MOBILIZING

The volatile situation in the Middle East has caused deep tension between Muslim and Jewish groups on college campuses around the United States. Dueling protests, defaced signs, and disrupted programs are all common occurrences. Some campus situations escalate so rapidly that police are called in, arrests are made, and student groups banned.

New York University has large populations of both Jewish and Muslim students, and neither group was shy about its point of view. So why have the two groups built peaceful, cooperative relations when Muslims and Jews on other campuses are frequently at each other's throats? The answer is that NYU has two interfaith leaders, Rabbi Yehuda Sarna and Imam Khalid Latif, who, while on opposite sides of many political issues, decided that there had to be a better way for Muslims and Jews to engage one another than shouting the other group down. The film *Of Many* by Linda Mills tells the story of how these two built a relationship of trust despite sharp differences, and leveraged their personal relationship to mobilize their respective communities in powerful interfaith projects.[5] What strikes me most about the story is how much skill, effort, and intention went into the process of building the relationship.

To begin with, they found common categories in which to ask each other questions and share their own stories. Some are harrowing. As a New Yorker, what was your experience of 9/11? Some are very specific to their own situation. How did you choose to become a leader in your faith community? Some are common to many. How did you ask your wife to marry you?

They recognized the importance of traveling to one another's religious institutions and sacred spaces. Khalid appears alongside Yehuda at a Jewish high school and gives a talk on the importance of understanding the narratives of people different than you. Yehuda comes to listen to Khalid preach at *jumma* prayers and accepts an invitation to come to the front of the congregation to offer a Jewish blessing.

They are able to bracket their differences and find other opportunities for collaboration. Yehuda attends a teach-in organized by the Muslim students on the hurt caused by the Danish cartoons that mocked the Prophet Muhammad. After the program is over, it is time for the evening prayer for Muslims, and Khalid leads the prayer right there on the street. Yehuda realizes that there is an appropriate Jewish prayer for this occasion. He stands alongside and prays in Hebrew as the members of the Muslim Student Association bend, kneel, and prostrate while chanting in Arabic. It is a signal of respect and relationship not lost on the gathering of Muslims.

Inevitably, as their relationship grows, violence breaks out again in the Middle East. Such moments have destroyed many budding interfaith relationships. It is easy to bracket differences when the issues at the center of those differences are not leading the evening news, and when people in your own religious community are not calling on you to vociferously side with your co-religionists. Denouncing the other group—including, and sometimes especially, your friends in that other group—is often viewed as the ultimate litmus test of loyalty to your community.

Khalid and Yehuda did not let the momentum of the negative event, or the strident voices of some in their respective communities, turn them around. Yehuda calls Khalid not long after the violence erupts and says that he hopes conflict between their communities on the other side of the world does not have a negative impact on their positive relationship building here. Khalid agrees. There is pressure to be quiet about their interfaith friendship, even to put it on the back burner.

They do the opposite. They go bigger instead of smaller. They become more public instead of more private. And instead of hashing out their views about the newest violence in the Middle East, they decide to mobilize their respective groups around other projects altogether, namely, service projects related to disaster relief. They make plans to travel to New Orleans after Hurricane Katrina and Joplin, Missouri, after a tornado ripped through the town. They organize groups of Muslim and Jewish students to join. They do service projects and speak with everyday citizens and leaders of local relief agencies. Soon, these Muslim-Jewish service trips become a regular occurrence at NYU. Not long after, Muslim and Jewish groups at other universities start doing the same.

How do Khalid and Yehuda mobilize enough people to shift the pattern of Jewish-Muslim relations at NYU from conflict to cooperation? They begin by building relationships with and involving the most influential members of their own religious communities, employing a version of the "first follower" dynamic illustrated in a classic YouTube video by Derek Sivers.[6] The "leader" in the Sivers video is a guy dancing alone at an outdoor festival. He could easily be dismissed as a nut, until one other person starts dancing with him. The initial dancer/leader embraces this first follower, shifting the attention to him, signaling to those seated, "Doesn't what this guy is doing just look *right* to you?" The leader recognizes that those seated have conflicting energies within them—the inertia of the existing pattern keeps them seated, but there is a desire to dance as well. The leader has to both relate and embody the story of dancing (note the resonances with

Gardner here), *and* to show that it is possible for others to follow this alternative pattern as well. He does this not by saying, "Follow me," but by getting a few other people to join and then effectively saying, "Follow them." Soon enough, the whole hillside in the Sivers video is dancing. Similarly, in the *Of Many* film, Khalid and Yehuda relate and embody the story of a new pattern of Muslim-Jewish relations on college campuses. They get the right first followers, and then many, many more follow those people.

So often the first instinct when it comes to mobilizing is to send out mass e-mails or put up colorful flyers advertising an event. That approach only works for football games and free food. With something as intimate and risky as an interfaith program, mobilizing a larger group is an extension of building personal relationships and relying on the first-follower dynamic. If you want a thousand people at an event that does not feature a celebrity, approach it by seeking to mobilize ten groups of a hundred, not by trying to reach a thousand separate individuals. To do that, you need to identify and build trusting relationships with the right ten people. These first followers will, in turn, energize the next wave.

CURATING INTERFAITH ACTIVITIES

It is instructive to watch the segments from *Of Many* in which the Muslim and Jewish students from NYU work together in New Orleans and Joplin. The first few sessions are tense. The warm relationship Yehuda and Khalid have developed played a role in getting the groups there, but it can't do all the work of melting the ice between them. Engaging in the activity itself has to accomplish that.

And that is exactly what happens. The common project of tearing down walls and putting up roofs creates a common bond. It is like watching Gordon Allport's intergroup relations theories in action. Muslims and Jews slowly break out of their same-religion groups and start to mix more freely, sharing personal stories, asking each other questions about their traditions, doing the kind of thing that Yehuda and Khalid have done for years.

The physical labor and the retreat environment create a powerful space. The Muslim students are impressed by how thorough the process is to make a kitchen kosher. The Jews are impressed that the Muslims wake up so early for the *fajr* prayer. They begin to pick up on similarities in their traditions that had gone previously unnoticed. A Muslim girl points out that ancient copies of both the Torah and the Qur'an were often rendered in gold paint. Working alongside the other group and then watching them pray has a powerful effect. As Yehuda notes, "Seeing each other in worship, in silence, as having sincere religious integrity and being willing to make some kind of self-sacrifice for the purpose of devotion, earned a kind of respect which was not easily dismissed."[7]

It also creates a space for emotional vulnerability. It is hard for Khalid to hold back his tears as he recalls the last night of the New Orleans trip, when a Jewish student approaches him and says, "In our tradition, when a rabbi walks into a room, we stand up out of respect. Going forward, anytime I'm sitting in a room and you walk into it, I'm going to stand up for you."[8]

Curating the right activity is a crucial skill of interfaith leadership. Unlike in grade school, where there are no bad questions, there *are* bad interfaith cooperation activities, and bad ways of organizing them. Bad interfaith activities exclude large groups of people by advancing divisive theological or political views. Bad interfaith activities guide conversations toward divisions rather than connections. Bad interfaith activities are ones that are boring.

Good interfaith activities bring together a wide range of people who orient around religion differently in compelling projects that highlight shared values and create the space for powerful sharing, storytelling, and relationship building. Good interfaith activities embody what William Vendley of Religions for Peace calls "values that are widely shared and deeply held." The pro-life position on abortion is deeply held but not widely shared, and therefore protests against abortion clinics (or, for that matter, in favor of them) do not make for good interfaith activities. Listening to esoteric lectures on arcane points of theology may be widely shared, but is not deeply held by enough people to make for an energizing activity. The best interfaith activities have participants saying, "I can clearly connect my faith to this project. I am inspired when I watch other people of different faiths connect to this activity. I can do this activity with diverse people. When we do these projects together, we find ourselves talking about our faiths in ways that deepen our connections to our own traditions and our relationships with one another."

Of all the various types of interfaith activities I have seen in the two decades I have done interfaith work, by far the most effective have been the kind of physically oriented service projects I've described, very often associated with Habitat for Humanity. Doing research on Habitat for Humanity one day, I learned that this intent was actually written into the original design. After several years as a successful businessman, Millard Fuller and his wife, Linda, decided to leave a life of affluence and go live at Koinonia, an ecumenical, interracial Christian work farm deep in Georgia. Millard, only a few months removed from being a successful corporate executive, spent his days packing pecans and milking cows with Koinonia's founder, Clarence Jordan, and developed there the "theology of the hammer" idea that became the heart of Habitat for Humanity.

The theology of the hammer includes the call to put one's deepest inspiration into action through service to others. But it also, crucially, involves creating activities and spaces that bring together people who otherwise disagree. At Koinonia, Fuller developed not only a commitment to proactively building interracial community, but also, at a time of deep division between various Christian denominations, ecumenical community. He writes, "Even though there may be strong differences on all sorts of things—baptism, communion, what night to have the prayer meeting, and how the preacher should dress, for example—we can agree on the imperative of the gospel to serve others in the name of the Lord."[9]

As Habitat went global, Fuller's vision expanded beyond Christian communities, including, as he writes, "Christian and Jew, Muslim and Hindu, Buddhist and Hindu, believer and infidel, totally devoted and entirely secular, friend of God and enemy of God."[10]

It worked for the Jews and Muslims at NYU. The relationships they built lasted long past their week of physical labor together. Back on campus, Muslim students began to frequent the Kosher Kitchen at NYU and Jewish students were seen hanging out at the Islamic Center. They did not agree on everything, but their disagreements no longer caused ugly divisions. As a female Jewish participant said,

> When you walk into a room with somebody and you've met them for the first time and you want to talk about the Middle East, you're going to start a screaming match, especially when you're on two different sides of the fence. You're going to yell at each other, you probably won't hear what the other person has to say, and you'll walk away and maybe never speak to that person again. But if they're your friend, if you've built that relationship through attending events, sharing meals together, doing service work side by side, you'll sit there and you'll listen. It may be really uncomfortable, you may completely disagree with what they have to say. But you'll listen. And you'll walk away as friends.[11]

FACILITATING INTERFAITH DIALOGUE

A few years back, I had the opportunity to spend two days doing interfaith workshops with students, faculty, and administrators at the University of Michigan at Dearborn. The midday session was with leaders from diverse religious student groups. I opened the workshop in the way diversity programs typically open, by stating that this would be a safe space where people could bring their whole selves. After a cursory review of some standard diversity discussion ground rules, I launched in: "Religion is too often left out of the diversity conversation. This afternoon, we are going to do something special and unique. We are going to talk openly about what is powerful for each of us about our faith."

Things pretty much went downhill from there.

The first comment came from an intense young man. He raised his hand and said, "I'm really grateful for a space where I can talk about my faith. It's the most important part of my life. I feel like there are always conversations about gender and race on campus, but never conversations about religion. One thing that's been bothering me a lot lately is how much this university is pushing homosexuality. You see it everywhere, and there is never a space for me to challenge that view and say that I as a Christian am called to love all people but also to call out what the Bible says is wrong."

He opened his mouth to start the next sentence, but I had heard enough. I cut him off and said, somewhat awkwardly, that we were not going to talk about that topic. I tried to move on to someone else, but the young man wanted to continue. "Can you talk about something else that's powerful about your faith?" I just about pleaded. He closed his mouth, folded his arms across his chest, and glowered at me.

Ten years into being a professional interfaith leader, I had committed an egregious, rookie mistake. Forgetting that the definition of religious diversity means deep disagreements on fundamental things, I had failed to properly guide the discussion with carefully crafted questions. Instead, I had stupidly assumed that when I invited people to share what was powerful about their faith identities, they would somehow naturally tell inspiring stories that pointed to common ground amid their differences and form themselves into an ideal little interfaith community that would serve as a model for the broader campus.

Just as diverse faith and philosophical communities do not magically mobilize themselves around activities that embody widely shared and deeply held values, neither do they wondrously share diverse perspectives and inspiring stories in a manner that builds community. Getting that to happen requires an interfaith leader skilled in the art of facilitating interfaith dialogue.

In other understandings of interfaith work, dialogue is the central activity, indeed, the main purpose for gathering. These are the models that view interfaith work as formal leaders of different world religions gathering together to discuss elements of doctrine, explain sacred rituals, or find agreement on ethics. In the approaches to interfaith work I present in this book—creating effective public health programs for religiously diverse communities, mobilizing various faith groups in disaster relief efforts—interfaith dialogue plays a somewhat different role. It almost always accompanies an activity, often in a kind of interfaith cooperation sandwich. There is dialogue in the mobilizing and design phase as the leadership group plans the activity, and there is some sort of formal, facilitated dialogue after the project takes place.

Much of the advice given to facilitators of diversity dialogues these days emphasizes creating a safe space for people to share their whole selves. Establishing ground rules is thought to be the most effective way to accomplish this. In the story of my own abysmal failure at the University of Michigan at Dearborn, I had made mention of the terms "safe space" and "whole self" and made at least a half-hearted attempt to establish ground rules. Still it was a disaster. Why? Because I had not been mindful of the single most important thing an effective facilitator does: ask the right questions.

My friend Rabbi Josh Feigelson helped me explore this theme further. He started an entire organization, Ask Big Questions, around the central insight that the key to getting diverse groups to have enriching conversations is to have trained facilitators guide discussions with good questions.

For a religiously diverse group of people who have just met, bad questions are ones that immediately start arguments ("What is your view on abortion?"), require specialized knowledge to answer ("What is the scientific consensus on when life begins?"), or simply don't matter enough to enough people.

Good questions actively guide interfaith conversations in useful directions. They are compelling to a wide range of people, evoke stories rather than opinions, and build connections across lines of difference rather than encouraging people to dig into entrenched, oppositional positions.

The best questions, in my view, help people deepen their relationships with their own traditions and their relationships with others at the same time—the very definition of interfaith work. The hope is to evoke the sharing of particular stories (meaning stories unique to specific faith and philosophical traditions) that approach widely held and deeply shared values. This is in sharp contrast to standard discussions about religion, which typically elicit oppositional arguments on divisive issues.

Interfaith discussion is most effective when an interfaith leader can play off a concrete activity the group has engaged in, leveraging the trust and goodwill that has already been established to encourage the group to engage in a question like "What from your tradition inspired you to participate in this Habitat for Humanity project?" Expert facilitators know how to hold up certain stories as models that others will follow, offering their own stories if compelling enough ones don't emerge quickly from the group. They know that a single question posed at the beginning of a session is unlikely to hold the group's attention for the entire time, so they are on the lookout for stories from the group that naturally will lead to other compelling questions. They allow the initial wave of natural leaders in the group to emerge, while at the same time creating space and issuing gentle invitations for quieter voices to share their stories. And they take special joy when one of those quieter voices winds up being a natural leader.

When that session at the University of Michigan at Dearborn finally, mercifully ended, the student I wrote about earlier approached me and said, politely but firmly, "That was not a safe space for my whole self."

He was right. I had made a tactical error by asking the wrong question at the beginning of the session, but I had committed an even graver sin by lying to him. That room was not a safe space for his whole self; it was not a safe space for *anybody's* whole self. A religiously diverse group of people will inevitably disagree on significant matters—the definition of marriage, the right to abortion, the rightful ownership of Jerusalem, questions regarding creation and salvation. A forceful expression of a view on one of these issues, which can certainly be said to be part of someone's whole self, may well lead another person to feel unsafe.

Interfaith leaders are trying to create a different kind of space, largely through the questions they ask and the conversation they facilitate. In my mind, it is even more inspiring than a safe space for people's whole selves, because such spaces require agreement and acceptance across the board, and that means the group gathered is really not diverse at all. That or someone is lying and either holding important things back or feeling uncomfortable and just not saying it.

I prefer an honest appraisal of reality. I prefer looking around a room and knowing how deeply I disagree with many of the people gathered on many things. But if we are mobilized around the right activity, if we are encouraged to talk about certain kinds of things in certain kinds of ways, we may feel an electric current of recognition; we may see ourselves as a community reflective of a religiously diverse democracy. Such a feeling is necessarily partial and contingent. In other situations, we may well find ourselves on opposite sides of a picket line. But I will know that those disagreements are also partial and contingent, that our widely shared and deeply held values are just as real as our arguments. Someone else may notice our ability to disagree on some fundamental things while working together on others. And they may tell the story of our relationship and offer it to the world as a public narrative, making us a stone in a bridge of interfaith cooperation.

QUALITIES

In any field, there are people who stand above the rest not because their knowledge or skills are that much better than everyone else's, but because they have intangible qualities that set them apart. The same is true for interfaith leaders. In this final chapter, I outline the qualities that I think mark truly exceptional interfaith leaders.

SEVEN

The Qualities of Interfaith Leadership

When I was in high school, I was a good enough basketball player to make the team my freshman and sophomore years, but not good enough to get very much playing time. Sitting on the sideline turned out to be a blessing in disguise. It gave me a lot of time to discern what traits separated the best players from the ones who were just good. Some of the separation was based on talent and work ethic, and some was based on knowledge of the game and hard basketball skills. But the longer I watched, the more I realized that what separated the best players from the merely good ones were some seemingly intangible qualities.

One way to illustrate this is to highlight the difference between doing well in practice and playing well during the game. Basketball practice is about growing your understanding and building your skills by breaking the game down into its component parts: rebound drills, three-man weaves, inbounds plays, and the like. We had players in practice who virtually owned individual drills, who would always win praise from the coaches ("Hey, run that drill over and this time go as hard as Fields."). But they could never quite put the whole thing together in the game. Truth be told, they looked like they were running a sequence of drills.

The best players, on the other hand, were masters of fluidity. They would go seamlessly from backpedaling on defense to a full-speed-ahead fast break, crashing into the lane at the perfect moment to grab the offensive rebound and get the score. They were always in the right place, anticipating where the action was rather than reacting to it. They had an uncanny sense of space and time, not only seeing the whole court but also having a feeling for the flow of the entire game, pacing themselves to last, finding bursts of energy when everyone else looked wiped out.

So much of this book has been like basketball practice, breaking interfaith leadership down into its component knowledge and skills parts. To be an effective interfaith leader, I think you've got to be pretty good at most of the parts I have described. But to achieve excellence, you need to create fluid motions out of these separate pieces, to think about the arc of years-long group processes alongside the guiding questions for individual sessions, to shift your energy at the drop of a hat from a person who insists that he has nothing in common with anybody of a different religion to someone who claims to agree with all religions and is frustrated that members of those religions refuse to agree with her.

In this final chapter, I will try to name those seemingly intangible qualities that separate excellent interfaith leaders from good ones. Qualities are hard to distinguish from skills. I suppose the difference for me is that a skill is something immediately obvious to everyone and relatively straightforward to practice. You can take classes in public narrative, mobilizing, and facilitating. There's money to be made in these things. Qualities are a little different. They are not immediately obvious to everyone; you have to be around a person for a long time to tease out the intangibles that account for her excellence. Also, you can't "practice" qualities the way you practice skills. Rather, you *cultivate* qualities by paying attention to them, the way someone who sits in meditation pays attention to her breath, committing to return to it after each scattering distraction.

GRIT

I begin with grit because I believe it is the foundational quality for effective interfaith leadership. You have to play the long game and know that you are going to encounter prejudice, tension, disagreement, and conflict along the way. Occasionally, this will be of the ugly sort. With some frequency, it will be directed at you. I once explained interfaith work to an editor at the *Chicago Tribune*. He laughed and said, "You're leading with your chin on the most divisive issue of our time." It occurred to me that this was a pretty good image. When you lead with your chin, you are inviting people to punch you. There are those who will happily oblige.

I remember heading in to speak to an evangelical student group on a campus in Minnesota and being warned that the members were angry about a Muslim being invited as the opening convocation speaker at their college, especially one who wrote a book supporting the Ground Zero mosque. One of them called my presence a "declaration of war." Did I go talk to them? I did. That was my punch on the chin for the week.

On another occasion, I was being given a tour of a Muslim education center by a senior Muslim leader who hailed from India. When he found out that India was the country of my birth as well, he took it as an opportunity to criticize Pakistan. "How can they call themselves a Muslim country," he railed, "when the founder, Muhammad Ali Jinnah, wasn't even a real Muslim." He stopped and turned to me and basically spat out with a sense of disgust, "He was an Ismaili." Then he turned around and continued walking.

Do I tell him that I'm an Ismaili? I wondered. Do I walk out, registering my offense? I continued with the tour and joined the group for prayer afterward. That was my punch on the chin for that week.

As I mentioned earlier, there is a trend in diversity work toward creating safety for people from marginalized identities. As someone who experienced no small amount of racism growing up and often felt that the powers that be around me (teachers, administrators) were totally oblivious to the verbal attacks that I was being subjected to, I appreciate many of the reasons behind the emphasis on safety. But there is no getting away from the fact that proactively engaging religious diversity will open you up to a range of beliefs, opinions, and views that will insult and offend you. Does a gay interfaith leader need to work with a Muslim imam who is vociferously opposed to same-sex marriage? Does a Muslim interfaith leader need to work with an evangelical pastor who pleads with her to take Jesus as her Lord and Savior so she can avoid the fire? It's not for me to say. Everybody draws their own lines. But anybody who does this work will need to be able to deal with some difference she doesn't like and even considers offensive. That takes a quality I'm calling grit.

RELATABILITY

When I was in my final year at the University of Illinois, I took a class in the sociology department that focused on the Latino experience. Unsurprisingly, the syllabus involved reading Latino history, novels, and essays, and class time focused on discussing themes that emerged from these texts. The majority of my classmates were Latinos, and also unsurprisingly, much of what they talked about was their experience as Latinos in the United States, connecting their lived reality with the assigned material.

I was going through a confrontational phase in my activist career and, for reasons that are a mystery to me now, I made it a point to raise my hand a couple of times every class and register the identity issues that were not being discussed. "How come there's no talk about Asian American issues?" I challenged my classmates one day. "What about gays and lesbians?" I asked the following week. "Have you entirely forgotten about black people?" I said at one point, acting incredulous. In each class, I mentioned a different identity or two. And in each class, I felt my classmates draw further and further away from me.

About midway through the term, the professor, a reserved and gentle man, called me up to his desk after class and said, "You make a series of interesting points, Mr. Patel. I wonder if you have noticed, however, that your classmates do not appear to be hearing what you are saying. Perhaps you would do better if you didn't come across as such a jerk." With that, he motioned to the door, dismissing me.

I am eternally grateful to that man; he taught me one of the most important lessons I learned in college. Self-righteousness will doom you. To be an effective social change agent, people have to want to listen to you. And for that to happen, you have to make yourself relatable.

The positive side of this coin is nicely illustrated in a story that Atul Gawande tells about a project called BetterBirth, whose purpose is to spread good childbirth practices in India.[1] The key agent in BetterBirth is a trainer working with delivery-room nurses to ensure the health of newborn babies. In addition to the basic knowledge and skills of better birthing practices, the key quality that effective BetterBirth staff exhibit is relatability.

Seema Yadav is a good example. Yadav's first assignment was to follow around an older nurse who had much more experience delivering babies than she did. During one particular birth, Yadav noticed that this nurse did not disinfect the room, check the pregnant woman's vital signs, wash her hands, or prepare emergency supplies. Instead of giving the newborn to the mother to warm skin to skin, she handed the baby to the relatives.

When Yadav pointed out areas of poor practice, the nurse seemed irritated and offered a litany of excuses. Yadav calmly walked through the best practices with the nurse, practices they both knew well, but that the nurse, in the chaos of delivering a baby in a challenging environment, simply didn't implement.

The next couple of times Yadav visited the nurse, not much had changed. She pointed out the lapses, and she also built the relationship. By the fourth and fifth visit, the best practices were starting to be implemented and the conversation between trainer and nurse had shifted as well. They shared cups of tea together and discussed why the various steps in the process were so important (you must wash your hands because gloves can have holes, and so on). The two exchanged cell phone numbers and began chatting in between visits, including about things not related to work, like their dreams for their families.

When Gawande heard the story, he wanted to talk to the nurse in person. It had been four months since Yadav's last visit, certainly enough time for the nurse to revert to bad habits. Over the course of the conversation, Gawande realized that the changes seemed to have stuck. The nurse walked through the best practices that were just part of her routine now. Before, she said, things were done haphazardly. Through the process of having Yadav at her side, "everything became more systematic."[2]

She had even put some of the steps into her own language. For example, to encourage mothers to do skin-to-skin warming with newborns, she told them that the uterus is very warm and when the baby comes out of the uterus, it wants to continue to be warm. The mother's skin helps with this.

Gawande wanted to know why an experienced nurse would listen to a much younger trainer. At first, the nurse admitted, she was not happy to have Yadav around. But soon she began to look forward to her visits.

"Why?" Gawande inquired.

"She was nice," the nurse said. "She smiled a lot. It wasn't like talking to someone who was trying to find mistakes. It was like talking to a friend."

In other words, it wasn't Seema Yadav's superior knowledge or skills that convinced the nurse to follow BetterBirthing practices; it was her quality of relating well to the nurse that caused and sustained the change.

LEADING WITH PLURALISM

In the early days of Islam, when the Muslim community was small and fledgling, and being harassed and hunted by the powerful tribes of Mecca, the Prophet Muhammad decided to send a contingent of his companions to a land called Abyssinia for their safety.

Why Abyssinia? Well, there reigned a ruler called the Negus. The Negus was a Christian, and the Prophet Muhammad believed that the faith of the Negus would move him to offer his protection to a small band of refugee Muslims.

When the Muslims arrived, the Negus called them to his court and demanded they explain themselves. They said they were Muslims, followers of the Prophet Muhammad, believers in the One God, reciters of a sacred scripture called the Qur'an. And then they began to recite the verses of the Qur'an that spoke of reverence for the Virgin Mary.

There are many ways that those Muslims could have explained their faith to the Christian king. They could have shaken their fists and marked their disagreement with the Christian belief that Jesus is the son of God. They could have wagged their fingers and lectured the Negus on the theology of prophethood in the Qur'an. Instead, they chose to highlight a dimension of their tradition that connected with a dimension of the tradition of the Negus.

I call this quality of choosing to highlight the inspiring things you have in common with another person or community "leading with pluralism." One of the best ways to lead with pluralism is to pay attention to the resonances between different traditions. It was a lesson I learned from father.

My dad was an MBA student at the University of Notre Dame in the mid-1970s, where he developed a fanatical devotion to Fighting Irish football. On autumn Saturdays when I was a kid, he and I would take I-90 out of Chicago into South Bend to go see Notre Dame football games. He'd point out the Golden Dome rising in the distance from the highway.

Our first stop was always the Grotto, a shrine to the Virgin Mary on the Notre Dame campus. We'd light candles and place them in the cove and stand for a few minutes in worshipful silence. By the time I was eleven or twelve, I realized there was something amiss in this scene. I was like, "Dad, aren't we Muslim? What are we doing standing prayerfully in front of a Catholic shrine?"

My dad pointed to the candles inside that cove and said, "The Qur'an describes God as light upon light." Then he put his hand on my shoulder and said, "Always look for the resonances."

These days, when I take my kids to Notre Dame football games, the Grotto is our first stop. My eight-year-old complains that he wants to get to the stadium instead of stop at this place where people are praying. I make him go anyway. I can't wait for the day when he asks me why we Muslims are praying at a Catholic shrine.

CRAFT

In his book *Shop Class as Soulcraft*, Matthew Crawford writes, "Craftsmanship means dwelling on a task for a long time and going deeply into it, because you want to get it right."[3] While Crawford is writing specifically about the mental and physical attention required for fixing motorcycles, reading his book helped me realize just how much craft matters in just about every calling in human life. The comics I love talk about the flow of the entire set and the importance of getting the timing of individual jokes just right. My favorite musicians talk about the imaginative worlds they want their music to create and the significance of the notes you *don't* play. Craft is not just about commitment to a particular endeavor; it's about knowing the things—big and little—you need to focus on to achieve excellence.

In his books *The Craftsman* and *Together*, the scholar Richard Sennett argues that the approach required to create a healthy community out of what might otherwise be just another group of squabbling humans is best understood as craft.[4] That is the way I see interfaith leadership.

I realize how peculiar it may seem to emphasize craft at the end of a book where the main metaphor is a feat of engineering and whose general approach has been pretty scientific—delineating outcomes, creating categories, defining terms, and the like. I guess it's because I believe all of those things are best approached in the light of craft.

What does it mean to understand interfaith leadership as a craft? Most important, it means you love the work—the discovery of interfaith histories, the polishing of interfaith narratives, the writing of new interfaith facilitation questions. You love it because you want to build a strong bridge to the beautiful destination of pluralism, to achieve the five civic goods of interfaith cooperation, to bring into community people who orient around religion differently. In other words, you love the ends.

But loving the work can never just be about achieving the ends. Surgeons don't expect to save every life; athletes know they are not going to win every game. If every loss is viewed as an irredeemable failure, you might never muster up the courage to start. At some level, you have to consider excellence in the process its own achievement. And you have to know that excellence in the process requires practice, what Sennett refers to as "sustaining habits."[5]

My friend Kevin Coval's life changed when he heard the poet Sonia Sanchez remark that a poet makes her bed every morning. Suddenly, what had long been a hobby to him, his writing, took on the shape of a craft. The morning after hearing Sanchez speak, Kevin woke at 7:23 a.m., made his bed, went to his desk, and started writing. His pen seemed possessed by the poetry spirits that morning. He viewed it as a sign. Every day since then, no matter how late he has been out the night before or where he is in the world, Kevin sets his alarm for 7:23, makes his bed, goes to his desk, and starts writing. Barely anybody sees Kevin doing any of this. They only see his electric public readings and his impressive number of books. But Kevin knows without the sustaining habit of that early morning writing session, none of those other things exist.

Nobody will see you hone your interfaith radar screen; they will only marvel at the range of stories in your public narrative. But if you aren't spending time behind the scenes collecting those stories, there is no way you can tell them. Nobody will see you map out the different directions an interfaith dialogue session might take; they will only marvel at how you came to ask the perfect facilitation question. They might never know that for every question you asked in that session, you had five more prepared that you didn't ask. Ten thousand hours of practice to achieve mastery, Malcolm Gladwell likes to say. People who approach their work as a craft feel privileged beyond belief that the universe has conspired to present them with this opportunity.

One final note on the question of craft as it relates to the central metaphor of this book, the bridge to pluralism. It is possible to collect the right stones, put them together in the right way, point them in the right direction, and still not have anybody show up wanting to cross. At the end of the day, people don't want to be halfway across a bridge, only to have it crumble underneath them. How do they know the bridge is strong enough and the destination is worth the risk? The answer is that they trust the bridge builder. In other words, the great secret to good leadership is very simple: people have to believe you. People will not believe you because you sell them on the beauty of the destination or the durability of the bridge. They will believe you because it is clear that you love your work, that you approach it with appropriate discipline and respect, that you have taken the time to acquire appreciative knowledge of their traditions, that you are able to articulate your own theology of interfaith cooperation, that a punch or two on the chin will not slow you down. They will risk the journey across the bridge, they will believe you, if it is apparent from the way you approach the craft of interfaith leadership that you believe yourself.

Conclusion

The Greater Chicago Food Depository occupies a football field–sized warehouse on the southwest side of the city. I visited one beautiful June morning and got a personal look at the boxes upon boxes of food stacked on the shelves, the trucks lined up to transport the food to needy people across the Chicago area, and the workers preparing meals for kids who qualified for free lunches. The size of the operation is both impressive and depressing, a monument to the moral scandal of hunger in a wealthy nation.

The CEO and a senior vice president of the Greater Chicago Food Depository, Kate and Steven, asked me to come in for breakfast and a conversation. Like many organizations that meet basic human needs, faith communities play a significant role in their work today. Over half of their food distribution centers are houses of worship or faith-based organizations, and many of the volunteer slots for activities like packing food for transport are filled by faith-based groups. As Chicago has grown more religiously diverse, the volunteer groups and food distribution sites have diversified as well.

For a long time, the organization's main strategy conversation revolved around improving its food supply chain and making its distribution systems more efficient. Basically some version of, how do we get more food to more hungry people more effectively?

But, especially in the wake of the 2008 recession, the number of hungry people kept growing and growing. Kate, Steven, and the Food Depository board were starting to ask a different question. Instead of addressing the ever-growing problem of hunger downstream, what might it look like to address it upstream? How could the Greater Chicago Food Depository shift some of the trends that were causing the hunger crisis in the first place?

As Steven and Kate watched the diverse religious volunteer groups come through their warehouse, often taking time for a moment of prayer and scripture reading before engaging in their volunteer work, they could not help but notice the similarities between these communities. Groups associated with faith communities were frequently the largest, the most consistent, the most creative, and the most effective partners of the Food Depository. Instead of simply asking more church groups to volunteer and more mosques to serve as food distribution sites, were there ways for the Food Depository to engage these groups in the more ambitious mission of seeking to end hunger in Chicago?

Ending hunger in Chicago would require policy changes. The Food Depository's most successful lobbying efforts to date had always involved religious leaders and congregations speaking to legislators in the state capitol. Ending hunger in Chicago would also require a change of heart. Too many Chicagoans who know where their next meal is coming from simply do not think enough about those who go hungry. Who better to speak to the moral scandal of hunger, and the sacred purpose of ending it, than diverse faith and philosophical groups?

As Kate and Steven discussed these questions, another thought occurred to them: What if various faith and philosophical communities came together on this project? How much more powerful would it be if busloads of Christians and Jews, Hindus and humanists, Muslims and Buddhists went together to the state capitol, rather than separately? What if the Food Depository could sponsor public-service announcements on local radio and television stations with Chicagoans of different religious backgrounds articulating their diverse faith and philosophical reasons for ending hunger? Wouldn't that approach have a better chance of changing more hearts in one of the most religiously diverse cities in the world?

Kate and Steven could see the potential so clearly. All of these different faith communities already partnered with the Food Depository.

When they came to pack food for distribution, they typically employed the same format: prayer, packing, scripture reading, facilitated discussion. They seemed game for just about anything—more volunteering, more fund-raising, more advocacy. But when Kate or Steven or someone else at the Food Depository suggested they work with other faith groups a little more, well, they weren't quite opposed to it, but it's not like the signup sheets were full.

A food metaphor was used: the ingredients for a great soup were all in the kitchen; they just weren't jumping into the pot. Kate turned to me. You run an interfaith organization, she said. Help us make this happen.

My answer was instant: you need to hire an interfaith leader.

You need to hire someone who has an appreciative knowledge of different religions, especially with regard to diverse religious ethics around hunger and poverty. More importantly, you need to hire someone with the skills to put that knowledge into action to mobilize those diverse groups. For some groups, this interfaith leader will be able to knock directly on the front door and talk to whoever opens it. For other groups, this person will need to tread more carefully, approaching them through the side door of references and trusted networks. A good interfaith leader will know which approach will work with what group.

Then this person will need to set up activities that bring these groups together. It may be that the first activities are closer to volunteerism than advocacy. Perhaps the Buddhists help package food with the Muslims, and the Catholics go to the food distribution center at the synagogue one Sunday afternoon. These "theology of the hammer" activities are attractive to a wide range of people.

A good interfaith leader knows that getting Buddhists and Muslims to serve together does not count as an interfaith activity—and won't get you to the next step—unless the faith of the participants is somehow involved. She will do something like break the two large faith groups into religiously diverse smaller groups, tell them to focus on the activity of packing food, and get to know one another through one simple question: tell me the story of your name. She knows that this will bring up people's faith in a fun, beautiful, animating way.

She sets aside forty-five minutes after the volunteer activity for an organized and facilitated interfaith discussion. She has made sure the leaders of the groups know that this is part of the program, so while some people grumble under their breaths, no one makes for the exits. Our interfaith leader is not thrown off by this rolling of the eyes; she just knows her facilitating has to be sharp and focused. People need to speak, listen, and learn. The question for interfaith discussion is simple: tell us a faith story that inspires you to serve those who are hungry. You can tell a story from the life of a great religious leader, or cite scripture, or just relate an example of a family member you felt exemplified the ethic of your tradition and community.

One thing our interfaith leader does not do is invite the groups to pray together. She knows that Muslims are focused monotheists and many Buddhists are nontheists, so she invites each group to do their prayer in faith-alike groups. Maybe later, they can figure out how to do it together, but on the first day, she judges separate prayer is a better choice.

Our interfaith leader spends her first few months setting up activities like those I've described just about every afternoon of the week. She knows she is not going to create a citywide interfaith antihunger campaign by personally facilitating food-packing afternoons. She needs dozens of these activities, and she needs them to slowly move up the chain of complexity from volunteerism to advocacy.

She spends her nights designing a twelve-module interfaith curriculum meant to push toward antihunger advocacy. Each week, there are prompts, questions, and short readings that are more theologically and socially challenging than the week before.

To get to scale, she is going to need to recruit and train a cadre of volunteer interfaith leaders—people who can mobilize, organize, and facilitate under her direction. Getting the right people is of paramount importance. Part of the reason she goes to all of the interfaith volunteer afternoons in the first few months is to get them started off right and to build trust with the participants. And part of the reason is to keep an eye out for budding interfaith leaders. By the end of the first three months, she's identified seven she thinks could make good trainers. She calls them all individually to request their participation. Five of them agree, and she organizes an afternoon-long training session that focuses on the larger goals of the campaign and the curriculum she has designed.

Three months later, her volunteers are going strong. She is able to turn her attention to power brokers in the city. She makes a list of the political, corporate, academic, philanthropic, and media leaders in town. She selects ten at the intersection of power, probable receptivity to message, and accessibility to her. She goes to see them armed with a clear message about the challenge of hunger in the city, the social capital potential of interfaith cooperation, and the opportunity to carry on the city's great history of interfaith work. She brings pictures of the interfaith volunteer work her groups are already doing every week to show momentum. She highlights results of the self-administered survey showing that over 80 percent of the participants report greater knowledge, better relationships, and more appreciative attitudes from the participation in the interfaith projects. She has a crisp request for each. Will the academic institutions host a conference focusing on creative ways to solve hunger? Will the philanthropists underwrite the conference? Will the mayor give opening remarks? Will media organizations air public-service announcements to encourage people to attend the conference?

At some point in my description, Kate and Steven stopped taking notes. I was talking too fast and, honestly, too much. "Sounds like you've been preparing for this conversation," Steven joked with me.

"Actually," I confessed, "I'm writing a book about this. You guys just got the executive summary, in full."

"Also," I added, "you just became the conclusion."

Kate chimed in, "The real reason we stopped writing is because we think you're right. We don't have anybody on staff to do this. We are going to need to hire someone."

I started ticking off various foundations that might support a grant for this kind of position. Kate interrupted me, saying, "This is important enough for us to do out of our operating budget. It's not a special project; it is core to our mission."

That comment silenced me. Here's the reason: I've been involved in interfaith work for almost two decades. I've served as founder and president of Interfaith Youth Core for fifteen years. This is the first time I've heard someone at a major organization say about something interfaith, "This isn't a special project; this is core to our mission. We need to put up the resources to do it right."

There are over two hundred food depositories in the United States. All of them rely on faith communities for volunteers and advocacy. All of those cities are becoming more religiously diverse as each day goes by. All of them would be excited about those diverse religious groups working together rather than separately. I'll bet you none of them are reaching their potential. I'll bet you food depositories are not the only places that have such potential.

The time for interfaith leaders has come.

Summary of Frameworks

(Page numbers are in parentheses.)

IDENTITY

Five Moments That Make Up an Interfaith Leader

- Moments of inspiration/enrichment from people or ideas of other traditions (30)
- Moments of connection/relationship with people or ideas of other traditions (32)
- Moments of prejudice/conflict regarding people or ideas of other traditions (32)
- Moments of action/cooperation with people or ideas of other traditions (33)
- Moments of recognizing difference with people or ideas of other traditions, and feeling admiration or appreciation despite those differences (34)

THEORY

The "Inter" in Interfaith: Levels of Interaction

- Individual identity (42)
- Continuity of religious communities (46)
- Microenvironments (51)
- Macroenvironments (56)

Ways to Respond to Diversity

- Barriers (63)
- Bunkers (64)
- Bludgeons (64)
- Bridges (64)

The "Faith" in Interfaith: Patterns of Orienting Around Religion

- World religions category (79)
- Intrafaith diversity (79)
- Intersectional identities (79)
- The religious nones (81)

VISION

Pluralism (91)

- Respect for identity (93)
- Relationships between different communities (93)
- Commitment to the common good (96)

The civic goods of interfaith leadership (97)

- Increasing understanding and reducing prejudice (98)
- Strengthening social cohesion and reducing the chances for identity-based conflict (98)
- Bridging social capital and addressing social problems (98)
- Fostering the continuity of identity communities and reducing isolation (99)
- Creating binding narratives for diverse societies (99)

The interfaith triangle (100)

- Knowledge (101)
- Attitudes (101)
- Relationships (101)

KNOWLEDGE BASE
- Appreciative knowledge (111)
- Theologies of interfaith cooperation (119)

- History of interfaith cooperation (126)
- Shared values (130)

SKILL SET

- Building a radar screen for religious diversity (135)
- Developing a public narrative of interfaith cooperation (139)
- Building relationships and mobilizing religiously diverse constituencies (142)
- Creating activities that bring people who orient around religion differently together (145)
- Facilitating interfaith conversations with a religiously diverse group (148)

QUALITIES

- Grit (156)
- Relatability (158)
- Leading with pluralism (160)
- Craft (161)

Acknowledgments

This book is a distillation of lessons and stories from my twenty years in interfaith work. It is only possible because of the unreasonable generosity of thousands of people I have met along the way. I wish I could thank you all.

There are many who played an active role in making this manuscript better. Several friends in the growing field of interfaith studies read drafts and made incisive comments that improved the final version. Thank you to Jacqueline Bussie, John Eby, Rahuldeep Gill, Paul Knitter, Jennifer Peace, and Or Rose.

Additionally, a circle of my colleagues at IFYC gathered for several sessions of constructive feedback on the book. Thank you to Nasser Asif, Tony Banout, Esther Boyd, Katie Bringman Baxter, William Campbell, Ben Correia, Pete de Kock, Mary Ellen Giess, Amber Hacker, Brendan Randall, Rebecca Russo, and Noah Silverman.

Thank you to my agent, Don Fehr, for helping me realize that the sudden insight I had one day could well be a useful book, and to my editor, Amy Caldwell at Beacon Press, for nurturing it from uneven fragments into a finished whole. Special thanks to my IFYC colleague Mesha Arant for assistance in research and formatting. The New World Foundation and the Hunt Alternatives Fund provided grants that gave me the necessary time and space to write this book, and the IFYC board gave me the opportunity to take that time and space to get the work done.

Finally, thank you to my wonderful wife, Shehnaz, and my two boisterous boys, Zayd and Khalil, for making living life even more fun than writing about it.

Notes

INTRODUCTION

1. J. David Goodman and Kirk Semple, "Another Silent Protest of Mayor de Blasio as Officer Liu Is Laid to Rest," *New York Times,* January 4, 2015, http://www.nytimes .com/2015/01/05/nyregion/police-officers-gather-for-the-funeral-of-wenjian-liu-killed -in-an-ambush.html.

2. G. K. Chesterton, *What I Saw in America* (orig. 1922; New York: Aeterna Press, 2014).

3. Adam Liptak, "Supreme Court Rejects Contraceptives Mandate for Some Corporations: Justices Rule in Favor of Hobby Lobby," *New York Times*, June 30, 2014, http://www.nytimes.com/2014/07/01/us/hobby-lobby-case-supreme-court -contraception.html.

4. John Rawls, *Political Liberalism* (New York: Columbia University Press, 1996).

5. Ibid.

6. Nicholas Wolterstorff, "The Role of Religion in Decision and Discussion of Political Issues," in *Religion in the Public Square: The Place of Religious Convictions in Political Debate* (Lanham, MD: Rowman & Littlefield, 2000), 105.

7. Martin E. Marty, *The One and the Many: America's Struggle for the Common Good* (Cambridge, MA: Harvard University Press, 1997).

8. Jeffrey Stout, *Democracy and Tradition* (Princeton, NJ: Princeton University Press, 2004).

9. Ibid., 298.

10. John P. Kotter, "What Leaders Really Do," *Harvard Business Review* (December 2001), https://hbr.org/2001/12/what-leaders-really-do.

11. Atul Gawande, "Slow Ideas: Some Innovations Spread Fast. How Do You Speed the Ones That Don't?," *New Yorker*, July 29, 2013, http://www.newyorker.com /magazine/2013/07/29/slow-ideas.

12. Ibid.

13. Everett M. Rogers, *Diffusion of Innovations* (New York: Free Press, 1962).

14. Gawande, "Slow Ideas."

15. Italo Calvino, *Invisible Cities* (Orlando, FL: Harcourt, 1974).

CHAPTER 1: THE IDENTITY OF AN INTERFAITH LEADER

1. David Bornstein, "The Barefoot Bank with Cheek," *Atlantic*, December 1995.

2. David Bornstein, "Changing the World on a Shoestring," *Atlantic*, January 1998.

3. Ibid.

4. Bill George, *True North: Discover Your Authentic Leadership* (San Francisco: Jossey-Bass, 2007).

5. Karl Simms, *Paul Ricoeur* (New York: Routledge, 2003).

6. Judith Plaskow, "An Accidental Dialoguer," in *My Neighbor's Faith: Stories of Interreligious Encounter, Growth, and Transformation*, ed. Jennifer Howe Peace et al. (Maryknoll, NY: Orbis Books, 2012), 77.

7. Walter Kirn, "Confessions of an Ex-Mormon," *New Republic*, July 13, 2012, https://newrepublic.com/article/104901/ex-mormon-romney-religion-kirn.

CHAPTER 2: THEORY: THE "INTER" IN INTERFAITH

1. Peter Berger, *The Many Altars of Modernity: Toward a Paradigm for Religion in a Pluralist Age* (Boston: De Gruyter Mouton, 2014).

2. Robert Putnam, "*E Pluribus Unum*: Diversity and Community in the 21st Century," 2006 Johan Skytte Prize Lecture, *Scandinavian Political Studies* (June 2007): 137–74.

3. Anthony Giddens, *The Consequences of Modernity* (Stanford, CA: Stanford University Press, 1990), 32.

4. Peter Berger, "Secularization Falsified," *First Things*, February 2008, http://www.firstthings.com/article/2008/02/002-secularization-falsified.

5. Jonathan Sacks, *The Persistence of Faith: Religion, Morality and Society in a Secular Age* (London: Weidenfeld and Nicolson, 1991), 32.

6. Diana Eck, *A New Religious America: How a "Christian Country" Has Become the World's Most Religiously Diverse Nation* (New York: Harper Collins, 2002).

7. Gordon Allport, *The Nature of Prejudice* (New York: Perseus, 1954).

8. Saul McLeod, "Robbers Cave," *Simply Psychology*, 2008, http://www.simplypsychology.org/robbers-cave.html.

9. Robert Putnam and David Campbell, *American Grace: How Religion Divides and Unites Us* (New York: Simon & Schuster, 2012).

10. Kim Severson, "For Some, Helping with Disaster Relief Is Not Just Aid, It's a Calling," *New York Times*, May 9, 2011, http://www.nytimes.com/2011/05/09/us/09baptist.html.

11. Samuel Huntington, "The Clash of Civilizations," *Foreign Affairs*, Summer 1993, 25.

12. Ibid., 27.

13. Ashutosh Varshney, *Ethnic Conflict and Civic Life: Hindus and Muslims in India* (New Haven, CT: Yale University Press, 2002), 12.

14. Robert Putnam, *Bowling Alone: The Collapse and Revival of American Community* (New York: Simon & Schuster, 2000), 66.

15. Ibid.

16. Robert Putnam, *Better Together: Restoring the American Community* (New York: Simon & Schuster, 2003).

17. Putnam, "*E Pluribus Unum*."

18. Eck, *A New Religious America*.

CHAPTER 3: THEORY: THE "FAITH" IN INTERFAITH

1. Wilfred Cantwell Smith, *Patterns of Faith Around the World* (Oxford, UK: Oneworld Publications, 1962), 21.

2. Ibid.

3. Paul Tillich, *Dynamics of Faith* (New York: Harper Collins, 1957).

4. Smith, *Patterns of Faith Around the World*, 24, 25.

5. Ibid., 27–28

6. Kenneth Crackwell, ed., *Wilfred Cantwell Smith: A Reader* (London: Oneworld Publications, 2002), 5–6.

7. Stephen Prothero, *God Is Not One: The Eight Rival Religions That Run the World* (New York: Harper One Publishers, 2001), v.
8. Ibid., 2.
9. Ibid., 4.
10. Karen Armstrong, "My Wish: The Charter for Compassion," TED video, February 2008, http://www.ted.com/talks/karen_armstrong_makes_her_ted_prize_wish_the _charter_for_compassion?language=en.
11. Will Herberg, *Protestant-Catholic-Jew: An Essay in American Religious Sociology* (Chicago: University of Chicago Press, 1955).
12. Robert Bellah et al., *Habits of the Heart: Individualism and Commitment in American Life* (Berkeley: University of California Press, 2007), 221.
13. Hans Küng, *Christianity: Essence, History, Future* (New York: Continuum, 1996), 105.
14. Putnam and Campbell, *American Grace.*
15. Susan Katz Miller, *Being Both: Embracing Two Religions in One Interfaith Family* (Boston: Beacon Press, 2013), xi–xii.
16. Molly Worthen, "Wanted: A Theology of Atheism," *New York Times*, May 30, 2015, http://www.nytimes.com/2015/05/31/opinion/sunday/molly-worthen-wanted -a-theology-of-atheism.html?_r=0.
17. Ronald Dworkin, *Religion Without God* (Cambridge, MA: Harvard University Press, 2013), 5.
18. Smith, *Patterns of Faith Around the World*, 13–16.
19. Mary Jo Bane, Brent Coffin, and Richard Higgins, *Taking Faith Seriously* (Cambridge, MA: Harvard University Press, 2005).
20. Karen Workman and Andrea Kannapell, "The Charleston Shooting: What Happened," *New York Times*, June 18, 2015, http://www.nytimes.com/2015/06/18/us /the-charleston-shooting-what-happened.html.
21. Nick Corasaniti, Richard Pérez-Peña, and Lizette Alvarez, "Church Massacre Suspect Held as Charleston Grieves," *New York Times*, June 18, 2015, http://www .nytimes.com/2015/06/19/us/charleston-church-shooting.html.
22. Ibid.
23. "Charleston Church Shooting: What Victims' Families Said to Dylann Roof," BBC News, June 19, 2015, http://www.bbc.com/news/world-us-canada-33185848.
24. Ibid.
25. John Eligon and Richard Fausset, "Defiant Show of Unity in Charleston Church That Lost 9 to Racist Violence," *New York Times*, June 21, 2015, http://www .nytimes.com/2015/06/22/us/ame-church-in-charleston-reopens-as-congregation -mourns-shooting-victims.html.
26. Eric Motley, "What I Learned in Bible Study: The Dialectical Dilemma of Love and Forgiveness—Reflections on Charleston," *The Aspen Idea Blog*, http://www .aspeninstitute.org/about/blog/what-i-learned-bible-study-dialectical-dilemma-love -forgiveness-reflections-charleston.

CHAPTER 4: THE VISION OF INTERFAITH LEADERSHIP

1. Eck, *A New Religious America.*
2. John Courtney Murray, *We Hold These Truths: Catholic Reflections on the American Proposition* (Oxford, UK: Roman & Littlefield Publishers, 1960), xiii.
3. Stout, *Democracy and Tradition.*
4. Anne Barnard, "As Trash Piles Up, So Does Contempt for Lebanon's Government," *New York Times*, August 27, 2015, http://www.nytimes.com/2015/08/28/world /middleeast/growing-trash-piles-reflect-lebanons-political-gridlock.html?_r=0.
5. Putnam and Campbell, *American Grace.*

6. See Christian Smith, *Soul Searching: The Religious and Spiritual Lives of American Teenagers* (New York: Oxford University Press, 2005).

7. Putnam, "*E Pluribus Unum.*"

8. Robert Bellah, "Civil Religion in America," *Dædalus: Journal of the American Academy of Arts and Sciences* 96 (1967): 1–21.

9. Putnam and Campbell, *American Grace.*

10. Ibid., 533.

11. Pew Research Center, "Muslims Widely Seen as Facing Discrimination," Pew Forum on Religious and Public Life, September 9, 2009, http://www.pewforum.org /2009/09/09/muslims-widely-seen-as-facing-discrimination/.

12. Gallup Center for Muslim Studies, "In U.S., Religious Prejudice Stronger Against Muslims," January 21, 2010, http://www.gallup.com/poll/125312/religious-prejudice -stronger-against-muslims.aspx.

13. Robert Wuthnow, *America and the Challenges of Religious Diversity* (Princeton, NJ: Princeton University Press, 2005).

CHAPTER 5: THE KNOWLEDGE BASE OF INTERFAITH LEADERSHIP

1. Paul F. Knitter, *One Earth Many Religions: Multifaith Dialogue and Global Responsibility* (New York: Orbis Books, 1995).

2. Ibid., 4.

3. Ibid., 5.

4. Stephen Prothero, *Religious Literacy: What Every American Needs to Know—And Doesn't* (New York: Harper One, 2007).

5. Ibid., 135.

6. Chaim Potok, *The Chosen* (New York: Ballantine Books, 1967).

7. Ibid., 175.

8. Ibid., 275.

9. Ibid., 188.

10. Ibid., 338.

11. Anne Fadiman, *The Spirit Catches You and You Fall Down: A Hmong Child, Her American Doctors, and the Collision of Two Cultures* (New York: Farrar, Straus and Giroux, 1997).

12. Alasdair MacIntyre, *After Virtue: A Study in Moral Theory* (Notre Dame, IN: University of Notre Dame Press, 2007), 250.

13. Brian McLaren, *Why Did Jesus, Moses, the Buddha, and Mohammed Cross the Road?* (New York: Jericho Books, 2013), 44.

14. Imam Ali Ibn Abi Taleb, *Nahjul Balagha*, Sermon 53.

15. Mahmood Jamal, *Islamic Mystical Poetry: Sufi Verse from the Early Mystics to Rumi* (New York: Penguin Classics, 2009).

16. Khaled Abou El Fadl, "The Place of Tolerance in Islam," in *The Place of Tolerance in Islam*, Khaled Abou El Fadl et al. (Boston: Beacon Press, 2002).

17. Ibid.

18. Umar Abd-Allah, "Mercy: The Stamp of Creation," Nawawi Foundation Paper, 2004, http://www.nawawi.org/wp-content/uploads/2013/01/Article1.pdf.

19. Ibid.

20. Abou El Fadl, "The Place of Tolerance in Islam."

21. Fazlur Rahman, *Major Themes of the Qur'an* (Chicago: University of Chicago Press, 1980).

22. Abou El Fadl, "The Place of Tolerance in Islam."

23. Umar Abd-Allah, "Islam and the Cultural Imperative," Nawawi Foundation Paper, 2004, http://www.nawawi.org/wp-content/uploads/2013/01/Article3.pdf.

24. Ibid.
25. Abou El Fadl, "The Place of Tolerance in Islam."
26. As an Ismaili, an important part of my own theology of interfaith cooperation is the emphasis that the Aga Khan, the leader of the Ismaili community, puts on building pluralism. The text of a speech he gave at Harvard in 2015, the Samuel L. and Elizabeth Jodidi Lecture, is one fine example: http://www.akdn.org/Content/1370 /Speech-by-His-Highness-the-Aga-Khan-Samuel-L-and-Elizabeth-Jodidi-Lecture-at -Harvard-University.
27. David Cannadine, *The Undivided Past: Humanity Beyond Our Differences* (New York: Alfred A. Knopf, 2013), 26.
28. Zachary Karabell, *Peace Be Upon You: Fourteen Centuries of Muslim, Christian, and Jewish Conflict and Cooperation* (New York: Vintage Books, 2008).
29. Kevin M. Schultz, "Protestant-Catholic-Jew, Then and Now," *First Things*, January 2006, http://www.firstthings.com/article/2006/01/protestant-catholic-jewthen -and-now.
30. Kevin M. Schultz, *Tri-Faith America: How Catholics and Jews Held Postwar America to Its Protestant Promise* (New York: Oxford University Press, 2011), 10.
31. Ibid., 41.
32. Ibid., 45.
33. Ibid., 41.
34. Herberg, *Protestant-Catholic-Jew*.
35. Paul F. Knitter, *Without Buddha I Could Not Be a Christian* (London: Oneworld Publications, 2009).
36. Ibid., 173.
37. Ibid., 176.
38. Ibid., 183.

CHAPTER 6: THE SKILL SET OF INTERFAITH LEADERSHIP

1. Madeleine Albright, *The Mighty and the Almighty: Reflections on America, God, and World Affairs* (New York: Harper Collins, 2007), 8–9.
2. Robert P. Jones, *The End of White Christian America* (New York: Simon & Schuster, 2016).
3. Howard Gardner, *Leading Minds: An Anatomy of Leadership* (New York: Basic Books, 2011), 14.
4. Marshall Ganz, "Why Stories Matter: The Art and Craft of Social Change," *Sojourners*, March 2009, https://sojo.net/magazine/march-2009/why-stories-matter.
5. *Of Many*, dir. Linda Mills (2014; New York: Spicy Icy Pictures and New York University, 2015).
6. "First Follower: Leadership Lessons from Dancing Guy," YouTube video, February 11, 2010, posted by "Derek Sivers," https://www.youtube.com/watch?v =fW8amMCVAJQ.
7. *Of Many*.
8. Ibid.
9. Millard Fuller, *The Theology of the Hammer* (Macon, GA: Smyth & Helwys, 1994), 7.
10. Ibid., 123.
11. *Of Many*.

CHAPTER 7: THE QUALITIES OF INTERFAITH LEADERSHIP

1. Gawande, "Slow Ideas."
2. Ibid.

3. Matthew B. Crawford, *Shop Class as Soulcraft: An Inquiry into the Value of Work* (New York: Penguin Press, 2009), 20.

4. Richard Sennett, *The Craftsman* (New Haven, CT: Yale University Press, 2008); and Richard Sennett, *Together: The Rituals, Pleasures and Politics of Co-operation* (New Haven, CT: Yale University Press, 2012).

5. Sennett, *The Craftsman*, 105.

Works Cited

Abd-Allah, Umar. "Islam and the Cultural Imperative." Nawawi Foundation Paper, 2004. http://www.nawawi.org/wp-content/uploads/2013/01/Article3.pdf.

———. "Mercy: The Stamp of Creation." Nawawi Foundation Paper, 2004. http://www.nawawi.org/wp-content/uploads/2013/01/Article1.pdf.

Abi Taleb, Ali Ibn. *Nahjul Balagha*, Sermon 53.

Abou El Fadl, Khaled. "The Place of Tolerance in Islam," in *The Place of Tolerance in Islam*, Khaled Abou El Fadl et al., Boston: Beacon Press, 2002.

Albright, Madeleine. *The Mighty and the Almighty: Reflections on America, God, and World Affairs*. New York: Harper Collins, 2007.

Allport, Gordon. *The Nature of Prejudice*. New York: Perseus, 1954.

Armstrong, Karen. "My Wish: The Charter for Compassion." TED video. February 2008. http://www.ted.com/talks/karen_armstrong_makes_her_ted_prize_wish_the_charter_for_compassion?language=en.

Bane, Mary Jo, Brent Coffin, and Richard Higgins. *Taking Faith Seriously*. Cambridge, MA: Harvard University Press, 2005.

Barnard, Anne. "As Trash Piles Up, So Does Contempt for Lebanon's Government." *New York Times*, August 27, 2015. http://www.nytimes.com/2015/08/28/world/middleeast/growing-trash-piles-reflect-lebanons-political-gridlock.html?_r=0.

BBC News. "Charleston Church Shooting: What Victims' Families Said to Dylann Roof." June 19, 2015. http://www.bbc.com/news/world-us-canada-33185848.

Bellah, Robert. "Civil Religion in America." *Dædalus: Journal of the American Academy of Arts and Sciences* 96 (1967).

Bellah, Robert, Richard Madsen, and William M. Sullivan. *Habits of the Heart: Individualism and Commitment in American Life*. Berkeley: University of California Press, 2007.

Berger, Peter. *The Many Altars of Modernity: Toward a Paradigm for Religion in a Pluralist Age*. Boston: De Gruyter Mouton, 2014.

———. "Secularization Falsified." *First Things*, February 2008. http://www.firstthings.com/article/2008/02/002-secularization-falsified.

Bornstein, David. "The Barefoot Bank with Cheek." *Atlantic*, December 1995.

———. "Changing the World on a Shoestring." *Atlantic*, January 1998.

Calvino, Italo. *Invisible Cities*. Orlando, FL: Harcourt, 1974.

Cannadine, David. *The Undivided Past: Humanity Beyond Our Differences*. New York: Alfred A. Knopf, 2013.

Chesterton, G. K. *What I Saw in America*. Originally 1922. New York: Aeterna Press, 2014.

Corasaniti, Nick, Richard Pérez-Peña, and Lizette Alvarez. "Church Massacre Suspect Held as Charleston Grieves." *New York Times*, June 18, 2015. http://www.nytimes .com/2015/06/19/us/charleston-church-shooting.html.

Crackwell, Kenneth, ed. *Wilfred Cantwell Smith: A Reader*. London: Oneworld, 2002.

Crawford, Matthew B. *Shop Class as Soulcraft: An Inquiry into the Value of Work*. New York: Penguin Press, 2009.

Dworkin, Ronald. *Religion Without God*. Cambridge, MA: Harvard University Press, 2013.

Eck, Diana. *A New Religious America: How a "Christian Country" Has Become the World's Most Religiously Diverse Nation*. New York: Harper Collins, 2002.

Eligon, John, and Richard Fausset. "Defiant Show of Unity in Charleston Church That Lost 9 to Racist Violence." *New York Times*, June 21, 2015. http://www.nytimes .com/2015/06/22/us/ame-church-in-charleston-reopens-as-congregation-mourns -shooting-victims.html.

Fadiman, Anne. *The Spirit Catches You and You Fall Down: A Hmong Child, Her American Doctors, and the Collision of Two Cultures*. New York: Farrar, Straus and Giroux, 1997.

"First Follower: Leadership Lessons from Dancing Guy." YouTube video, February 11, 2010. Posted by "Derek Sivers." https://www.youtube.com/watch?v=fW8amMCVAJQ.

Fuller, Millard. *The Theology of the Hammer*. Macon, GA: Smyth & Helwys, 1994.

Gallup Center for Muslim Studies. "In U.S., Religious Prejudice Stronger Against Muslims." January 21, 2010. http://www.gallup.com/poll/125312/religious-prejudice -stronger-against-muslims.aspx.

Ganz, Marshall. "Why Stories Matter: The Art and Craft of Social Change." *Sojourners*, March 2009. https://sojo.net/magazine/march-2009/why-stories-matter.

Gardner, Howard. *Leading Minds: An Anatomy of Leadership*. New York: Basic Books, 2011.

Gawande, Atul. "Slow Ideas: Some Innovations Spread Fast. How Do You Speed the Ones That Don't?" *New Yorker*, July 29, 2013. http://www.newyorker.com /magazine/2013/07/29/slow-ideas.

George, Bill. *True North: Discover Your Authentic Leadership*. San Francisco: Jossey-Bass, 2007.

Goodman, J. David, and Kirk Semple. "Another Silent Protest of Mayor de Blasio as Officer Liu Is Laid to Rest." *New York Times*, January 4, 2015. http://www.nytimes .com/2015/01/05/nyregion/police-officers-gather-for-the-funeral-of-wenjian-liu -killed-in-an-ambush.html.

Giddens, Anthony. *The Consequences of Modernity*. Stanford, CA: Stanford University Press, 1990.

Herberg, Will. *Protestant-Catholic-Jew: An Essay in American Religious Sociology*. Chicago: University of Chicago Press, 1955.

Huntington, Samuel. "The Clash of Civilizations." *Foreign Affairs*. Summer 1993.

Jamal, Mahmood. *Islamic Mystical Poetry: Sufi Verse from the Early Mystics to Rumi*. New York: Penguin Classics, 2009.

Jones, Robert P. *The End of White Christian America*. New York: Simon & Schuster, 2016.

Karabell, Zachary. *Peace Be Upon You: Fourteen Centuries of Muslim, Christian, and Jewish Conflict and Cooperation*. New York: Vintage Books, 2008.

Katz Miller, Susan. *Being Both: Embracing Two Religions in One Interfaith Family*. Boston: Beacon Press, 2013.

Knitter, Paul F. *One Earth Many Religions: Multifaith Dialogue and Global Responsibility*. New York: Orbis Books, 1995.

———. *Without Buddha I Could Not Be a Christian*. London: Oneworld, 2009.

Kotter, John. "What Leaders Really Do." *Harvard Business Review*, December 2001. https://hbr.org/2001/12/what-leaders-really-do.

Kirn, Walter. "Confessions of an Ex-Mormon." *New Republic*, July 13, 2012. https://newrepublic.com/article/104901/ex-mormon-romney-religion-kirn.

Küng, Hans. *Christianity: Essence, History, Future*. New York: Continuum, 1996.

Liptak, Adam. "Supreme Court Rejects Contraceptives Mandate for Some Corporations: Justices Rule in Favor of Hobby Lobby." *New York Times*, June 30, 2014. http://www.nytimes.com/2014/07/01/us/hobby-lobby-case-supreme-court-contraception.html.

MacIntyre, Alasdair. *After Virtue: A Study in Moral Theory*. Notre Dame, IN: University of Notre Dame Press, 2007.

Marty, Martin E. *The One and the Many: America's Struggle for the Common Good*. Cambridge, MA: Harvard University Press: 1997.

McLaren, Brian D. *Why Did Jesus, Moses, the Buddha, and Mohammed Cross the Road? Christian Identity in a Multi-Faith World*. New York: Jericho Books, 2013.

McLeod, Saul. "Robbers Cave." *Simply Psychology*, 2008. http://www.simplypsychology.org/robbers-cave.html.

Motley, Eric. "What I Learned in Bible Study: The Dialectical Dilemma of Love and Forgiveness—Reflections on Charleston." *The Aspen Idea Blog*. http://www.aspeninstitute.org/about/blog/what-i-learned-bible-study-dialectical-dilemma-love-forgiveness-reflections-charleston.

Murray, John Courtney. *We Hold These Truths: Catholic Reflections on the American Proposition*. Oxford, UK: Roman & Littlefield, 1960.

Of Many. Film. Directed by Linda Mills. 2014. New York: Spicy Icy Pictures and New York University, 2015.

Pew Research Center. "Muslims Widely Seen as Facing Discrimination." Pew Forum on Religious and Public Life, September 9, 2009. http://www.pewforum.org/2009/09/09/muslims-widely-seen-as-facing-discrimination/.

Plaskow, Judith. "An Accidental Dialoguer." In *My Neighbor's Faith: Stories of Interreligious Encounter, Growth, and Transformation*. Edited by Jennifer Howe Peace, Or N. Rose, and Gregory Mobley. Maryknoll, NY: Orbis Books, 2012.

Potok, Chaim. *The Chosen*. New York: Ballantine Books, 1967.

Prothero, Stephen. *God Is Not One: The Eight Rival Religions That Run the World*. New York: Harper One, 2001.

————. *Religious Literacy: What Every American Needs to Know—And Doesn't*. New York: Harper One, 2007.

Putnam, Robert. *Better Together: Restoring the American Community*. New York: Simon & Schuster, 2003.

————. *Bowling Alone: The Collapse and Revival of American Community*. New York: Simon & Schuster, 2000.

————. "*E Pluribus Unum*: Diversity and Community in the 21st Century." 2006 Johan Skytte Prize Lecture. *Scandinavian Political Studies* (June 2007).

Putnam, Robert, and David Campbell. *American Grace: How Religion Divides and Unites Us*. New York: Simon & Schuster, 2012.

Rahman, Fazlur. *Major Themes of the Qur'an*. Chicago: University of Chicago Press, 1980.

Rawls, John. *Political Liberalism*. New York: Columbia University Press, 1996.

Rogers, Everett M. *Diffusion of Innovations*. New York: Free Press, 1962.

Sacks, Jonathan. *The Persistence of Faith: Religion, Morality and Society in a Secular Age*. London: Weidenfeld and Nicolson, 1991.

Schultz, Kevin M. "Protestant-Catholic-Jew, Then and Now." *First Things*, January 2006. http://www.firstthings.com/article/2006/01/protestant-catholic-jewthen -and-now.

————. *Tri-Faith America: How Catholics and Jews Held Postwar America to Its Protestant Promise*. New York: Oxford University Press, 2011.

Sennett, Richard. *The Craftsman*. New Haven, CT: Yale University Press, 2008.

————. *Together: The Rituals, Pleasures and Politics of Co-operation*. New Haven, CT: Yale University Press, 2012.

Severson, Kim. "For Some, Helping with Disaster Relief Is Not Just Aid, It's a Calling." *New York Times*, May 9, 2011. http://www.nytimes.com/2011/05/09/us/09baptist .html.

Simms, Karl. *Paul Ricoeur*. New York: Routledge, 2003.

Smith, Christian. *Soul Searching: The Religious and Spiritual Lives of American Teenagers*. New York: Oxford University Press, 2005.

Smith, Wilfred Cantwell. *Patterns of Faith Around the World*. Oxford, UK: Oneworld Publications, 1962.

Stout, Jeffrey. *Democracy and Tradition*. Princeton, NJ: Princeton University Press, 2004.

Tillich, Paul. *Dynamics of Faith*. New York: Harper Collins, 1957.

Varshney, Ashutosh. *Ethnic Conflict and Civic Life: Hindus and Muslims in India*. New Haven, CT: Yale University Press, 2002.

Wolterstorff, Nicholas. "The Role of Religion in Decision and Discussion of Political Issues." In *Religion in the Public Square: The Place of Religious Convictions in Political Debate*. By Nicholas Wolterstorff and Robert Audi. Lanham, MD: Rowman & Littlefield, 2000.

Workman, Karen, and Andrea Kannapell. "The Charleston Shooting: What Happened." *New York Times*, June 18, 2015. http://www.nytimes.com/2015/06/18/us/the -charleston-shooting-what-happened.html.

Worthen, Molly. "Wanted: A Theology of Atheism." *New York Times*, May 30, 2015. http://www.nytimes.com/2015/05/31/opinion/sunday/molly-worthen-wanted-a -theology-of-atheism.html?_r=0.

Wuthnow, Robert. *America and the Challenges of Religious Diversity*. Princeton, NJ: Princeton University Press, 2005.

Index